myths, legends, and realities

The Perfect Life

of

LOVERS

people

places

expressions of love

myths, legends, and realities

The Perfect Life

of

LOVERS

people

places

expressions of love

by

Monique Pivot

BARRON'S

MYTHS, LEGENDS, AND REALITIES

6

PEOPLE

34

1

2

PLACES

62

EXPRESSIONS OF LOVE

88

MYTHS, LEGENDS, AND REALITIES

MYTHS, LEGENDS, AND REALITIES

C ould it be that love is only a myth, a legend that sweeps people's aspirations on toward a utopian fusion between two beings and nothing more than a product of their imaginations? Is it instead the intangible reality that some people, such as poets, proclaim aloud from on high? If so, the myth is perhaps nothing more than a symbol of the perfect union of two beings, which gives it substance. Whatever the case, love—an inaccessible dream or a contingent reality—is undeniably as essential to us as the air we breathe.

Is love a human invention, or is it more likely of divine origin? Ever since ancient times, gods and goddesses have seemed to live exclusively in the service of love in all its forms. Does that mean that the god of love presides over the existence and the perpetuation of the human species? Yes if you associate love with nothing more than the reproduction of the species, but that fails to take into account a number of legendary couples. No if we consider that love is something quite different and beyond the union of physical bodies—

an impulse, a fusion, a vow to love forever. For a long time, being in love did not even seem necessary to get married and have children. The church, in particular, took a dim view of that. Nowadays, love is king. Everything else counts for little. The misfortune of some makes for the happiness of others—and vice versa—and we witness the triumph of love. Love is a daily reality, within reach and accessible to desire. In this first part of *The Perfect Life*, we present how people have professed their love through the ages. We show the different types of love, from courtly love, to criminal passion, to mythical couples, those who constructed and who continue to uphold the legends, plus how lovers live and feed their passion, sometimes with eccentricities that are amusing, silly, or tragic. You'll see that love can be as easy as saying hello—or better yet, goodnight—and as complicated as life itself. "All's well that ends well," or "They lived happily and had lots of children" is the way most fairy tales about love end. Is this the reality of the legend or the legend of the reality? Let's have a look. . . .

From left to right:
The Return of Ulysses by Corazzelli Guidoccio (1450–1516/1517). Ulysses is reunited with his faithful Penelope.
National Renaissance Museum, Ecouen.
The Prince despairs as Cinderella leaves the ball.
The Goblin Factory, after a cartoon by Jean Veber.
A poet in the presence of his lady. Illustration of courtly love.
Miniature from the fourteenth century.
Josette Day and Jean Marais in *Beauty and the Beast*; beauty in opposites (Jean Cocteau film, 1946).

The History of Love Throughout the Ages

Love is as old as human history. In the oldest myths of antiquity, it is evoked through the god Eros as a principle of life and as the desire for fertility. Just like laughter, love is a property of humankind. How could we imagine Adam and Eve indifferent to one another—surely it was the experience of their love that drove them from Paradise—or founding myths without the certainty of love's reality? Religion can scarcely be imagined without love of God or a mystical impulse.

In early times, courtship must have been rather scanty unless one belonged to a noble family. Asking for the hand of a girl involved respect for her virtue and a few letters containing perhaps a little eroticism. This was a carefully disguised eroticism mixed with poetry, a bouquet of flowers here and there, and an engagement ring—but with a minimum of effusiveness.

Here are some specific instances: Tristan and Isolde braved the wrath of King Mark. Eloise secretly wed her tutor Abélard in defiance of her uncle, the canon Fulbert, who subsequently had the brilliant young theologian emasculated. Lancelot of the Lake accepted all kinds of sacrifices in order to seduce the wife of his sovereign, King Arthur, and Guinevere yielded to the knight's advances.

Courtly love as it was practiced in the Middle Ages remains a model of the genre. It was widespread mainly in Provence and southern France, where prejudices were less confining than in the north. Troubadours imposed upon themselves a whole series of trials to win the heart of a young lady, generally of noble birth. Most of the time, though, all they got as recompense for this devotion was a simple kiss—nothing very dramatic by our standards but quite bold for the time.

In the eleventh century, William IX of Aquitaine, a grand lord and great libertine (who was even excommunicated), sang the despair of the chivalrous troubadour:

Etruscan sarcophagus. The husband gently holds his wife in a protective gesture.
The Louvre, Paris.

The Novel of Galahad the Knight, Tristan and Lancelot. Tristan, disguised as a crazy man, is reunited with Isolde in Cornwall.
Condé Museum, Chantilly.

Sixteenth-century couple. Engraving according to Goltzius. Lusty gazes and bold gestures. The eyes tell the story. . . .
National Library of France, Paris.

High-class lady walking with courtier (seventeenth century). Engraving by Nicholas Arnoult.
National Library of France, Paris.

"... My lady tries me and tests me to find out how I love her: but never, no matter what kinds of quarrels she picks with me, will I ever release myself from her bondage. ...

... What will you gain, lovely woman, if you distance me from our love? It seems you want to become a nun. You must know that my love is such that I fear death by heartache if you do not repair the injustices that give rise to my complaints. ..."

Ronsard celebrates his unrequited love, or more precisely, loves, for the three women to whom he dedicates his most beautiful verse, Cassandra Salviati, Marie Dupin, and Hélène de Surgères. To Cassandra he writes:

> Blessed be my worsening torments
> And the sweet yoke that makes me sigh;
> Blessed be my worried mind.
> Blessed be her sweet remembrance,
> And happier still the wrath from her eyes
> That sears my life in fire that freezes me to ice.

To Marie he writes:

> My soul is so smitten by a bed of regret
> That never again will I stray
> Near that chamber of love, let alone the bed
> Where I saw my mistress last May.

"Ronsard celebrates love, or more precisely, his loves."

The aging Ronsard addresses Hélène. He knows full well that the young and much-courted beauty will never fall into his arms, and he sheds tears over his own white hair:

> I can never return to the springtime of my life
> Please love me, though I am gray,
> And I'll love you when you're the same way.

Above:
The plot of
Clélie, a novel by
Madeleine de Scudéry
(1607–1701), unfolds against the
background of a map of Tender,
an allegorical land of love.
Inset:
A gentleman takes leave of a
high-class lady. Engraving by
Launay, after Moreau, Jr. (1777).
National Library of France, Paris.

In the Mill Street Salon by Henri de Toulouse-Lautrec (1864–1901). The wooden expressions of the women at different stages in life express their despair.
Albi Museum.

At this time, Louise Labé (1524–1566) takes up the long erotic tradition so well represented by the medieval troubadours such as Jean Bodel d'Arras and Gautier Le Leu and by poets like Clément Marot.

> *Kiss me, keep kissing, and kiss again:*
> *Give me your tastiest kiss,*
> *Most filled with lovers' bliss:*
> *The ones I return will be hotter than coals . . .*
> *Let us mix our happy kisses*
> *And enjoy one another at leisure.*

"Let us mix our happy kisses And enjoy one another at leisure."

In the classical period, love occupies the high ground in the salons as well as in literature. Mademoiselle de Scudéry draws up her map of Tender. The pastoral genre thrives. Noble and heroic love bursts forth in alexandrine verse on stage at the theater and the opera.

After the Romanesque writers, the romantics extol in prose and verse the virtues of discreet courtship, filled with nuances and halftones, with strolls and epic horseback rides.

In the *Poetic Meditations* of Lamartine, dedicated to Elvira at the theater of Musset, lovers gaze into each other's eyes, find ways to slip away, and exchange vows and promises. However, they also abandon themselves to passion, even to excess and despair.

By using trifles in the form of love notes and declarations on bended knee prior to embracing, the nineteenth and especially the twentieth centuries manage to admit that love is not merely an affair of the head and heart. In fact, today the term *courtship* has lost most of its meaning and seems laughable.

Who knows, though? In the near future, maybe this gallant custom will come back into fashion one way or another. We shall see.

The Strollers by Claude Monet (1840–1926). Elegance and restraint are reflections of love.
Washington Museum.

What is love's fate in a blue-collar world demeaned by alcohol during the time of Emile Zola (1840–1902)?
Museum of Decorative Arts.

MYTHICAL COUPLES

Whether they're real or put together from loose parts, mythical couples haunt our imagination and our collective consciousness. Adam and Eve, Orpheus and Eurydice, Philemon and Baucis, Ulysses and Penelope, and Tristan and Isolde—they all mean something to us and serve as examples, even if only unconsciously.

Adam and Eve by Albrecht Dürer (1471-1528). Natural beauty from the time before original sin.
The Prado, Madrid.

Venus and Love Sleeping by Jean-Baptiste Regnault (1754-1829), engraved by Cazenave. The innocence of love unperturbed by the sensuousness of the flesh.

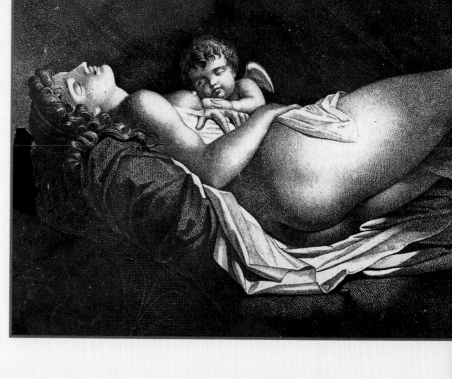

Letters of Héloïse and Abélard, engraved by Jean-Michel Moreau the younger (1741-1814). The lovers realize their transgression against religious edict.
National Library of France, Paris.

Paul and Virginie, a famous 1788 novel by Bernadin de Saint-Pierre, introduces a virtuous couple totally at odds with the exotic, luxuriant background more suited to voluptuous love. National Museum of Arts from Africa and Oceania, Paris.

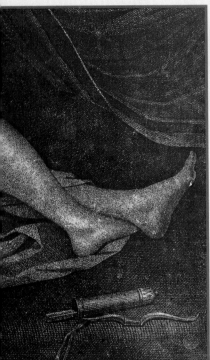

Jupiter and Mercury with Philemon and Baucis by Jacob Jordaens (1593–1678). This legend illustrates the duty of hospitality and fidelity in marriage. Atheneum, Helsinki.

In *The Red and the Black*, a 1954 movie adaptation of Stendahl's novel, Claude Autant-Lara introduces an unforgettable couple: Gérard Philippe and Danielle Darrieux. Love transcends social differences and bourgeois morality.

Love as an Eternal Refuge

"What good is love—love's good for nothing," sang Edith Piaf with great conviction and plenty of success—and without generating much controversy. No lovers on earth have ever been concerned about the finality of their love. Passion directed toward another person, unique and irreplaceable, is well-known; no need to ask questions on that score. "There are sixty queens, eighty concubines, and countless young girls. But only one of them is my dove, my perfection; she's the only one;" the chant sounds like an echo of The Song of Solomon.

In ancient Greece, love was "given" by the gods, and the object of one's love became a reflection of divine perfection. At the same time in Rome, Ovid sang the praises of good company in his *Loving* and *The Art of Loving*. From the loves of the Bible to the "better half" mentioned by Jean-Louis Bory, the main object is finding the one person who was made for you. All the rest, including marriage, is nothing more than literature. This unique person may be unique for life, for several days, or a few months. It matters not: the *other person* makes it possible to form a couple and project it enduringly into the future.

"Happy people seemingly have no tale to tell."

Throughout the ages, love has inspired artists, who have regarded it differently depending on whether they are telling their own story or someone else's. ("Madame Bovary is me," Flaubert asserted.) Happy people seemingly have no tale to tell. Painters, sculptors, writers, and musicians all have one, and it rarely ends happily.

From Dante to Aragon and Chrétien de Troyes to Leo Ferré, lovers have not always enjoyed the blessings of fate. Just the same, they have experienced exaltation, delay, a burning in their soul and senses, and the certainty that it *will* last forever. For love is an eternal refuge, a cocoon to which lovers turn to protect their happiness or assuage their misery.

There's no need to mention that an infinite amount has been written on the topic of love. For centuries, there's been just one way to express one's feelings: writing. Poems, letters, notes, and literature are filled with

The Divine Comedy (1307–1321) by Dante is illustrated here by the Venetian school. Beatrice leads Dante to Paradise where he meets the saints. Love has led Dante toward divine benediction.

The Morning Hymn at Bach's, engraving by Biscombe-Gardner after Rosenthal. The domestic happiness that comes from having a large family.

. . . Love Poems

The less I see her, the more her do I hate;
The more that I despise her, the less am I irate.
The more I love her, the less to me it means;
The more I flee her, the sweeter her esteem.
Conflicting forces are my fate,
Boredom with pleasure, love, and hate.
Strong is the love that keeps me bound
When hate and vengeance come around:
I then detest with vain desires
The very one my heart requires.
Maurice Scève, *Delia*, 43, 1544.

I live in you, no matter you're away;
I die in me, wherever I may stay.
Absent you may be, but present yet you are;
Near am I, but still remain afar.
And if nature insult felt
Because too much in you I've dwelt,
The high power that opens gently,
Infuses my soul into this base body,
Strips it of its essence,
And imparts it to you in its highest form.
Maurice Scève, *Delia*, 144, 1544.

declarations and vows. The plays of Musset, Marivaux, and Tennessee Williams are nothing but love stories with a few added side trips.

When he declared that *Love Is Not a Trifling Matter*, Musset was giving vent to the pain he felt from his break with George Sand. Shakespeare, in *A Midsummer Night's Dream*, *Romeo and Juliet*, and *Othello*, is hardly any happier; nor is Tennessee Williams (*Cat on a Hot Tin Roof*, *A Streetcar Named Desire*, and others).

Even Marivaux—even if his work really is more substantial than just pleasant, affected banter. He presents love's more comical side in *The Double Deception* and *The Game of Love and Chance*. Likewise, Beaumarchais, while he encourages Chérubin's love for the countess Almaviva in *The Marriage of Figaro*, is dealing with something quite different from love. Classics, romantics, and contemporaries use and abuse love and lovers. Nothing delights a poet or a writer more than the story of a romantic adventure. Think of Stendhal and his *The Red and the Black* and *About Love* (both essay and autobiography); Goethe and his *Song of May*, *Welcome*, and *Goodbye*; Valery Larbaud (*Lovers, Happy Lovers*); and Apollinaire with the *Song of the Unloved*:

"Nothing delights a poet or a writer as much as the story of a romantic adventure."

> . . . *When he finally returned*
> *To his land, wise Ulysses'*
> *Old dog remembered him*
> *Near an old high-warp tapestry*
> *His wife awaited his return.*
>
> *The royal spouse of Sacontale (1)*
> *Tired of conquering rejoiced*
> *When he found her pale*
> *From waiting and eyes glassy with love*

(1) *Heroine of an Indian story (fifth century* A.D.*), renowned for her faithfulness.*

Caressing her pet gazelle
I thought of those happy kings
When false love and the one
That I still love
Striking their faithless shadows
Made me so unhappy.

In *Adolphe*, Benjamin Constant wrote: "Love is so much identified with its object that there is a certain charm even in despair. It struggles against reality, against fate; the ardor of its desire gives a false picture of its strength and exalts it in the middle of its pain."

Here's what Paul Eluard had to say in *The Alliance*:

They are two small trees
Alone in a field
They will always be together.

Jacques Prévert wrote in *Adonides*:

I am happy
Yesterday he told me
That he loves me
I am happy and proud
And free as a bird
He failed to add
That it's forever.

All these authors expose happiness, misery, joy, hope, and passion until death, as in *Belle du Seigneur* by Albert Cohen. Love in all its states. . . . Painters have not experienced the same freedom of inspiration and tone. For a long time, only religious or allegorical themes were sanctioned: Venuses and Cupids suggest and stand for love, but never a couple. As for portraits, they are more often commissioned pieces than celebrations of the woman loved, even if painters commonly fell in

Verdi, in Florence in 1847, composing a production of *Macbeth*, thinks of a role for the famous soprano Guiseppina Strepponi (below) who would become his wife.

love with their models. We had to wait until Picasso for an artist to paint the women in his life. Dali painted Gala, and Bernard Buffet painted Annabel.

Many great musicians have been unhappy in love. Exceptions include Wagner, who found fulfillment in his marriage to Cosima, Liszt's daughter; Schumann, who finally managed to wed his Clara after numerous difficulties; and the ebullient Verdi, whose liaison with Miss Strepponi, his favorite singer, had a positive influence on his work. Many of these composers created lasting masterpieces. Beethoven knew little more than fond friendships and an equal number of disappointments of the heart. (It will never be known for whom the letter to the "Immortal Beloved" was intended.) Just like Schubert, he was ill-served by his unattractive appearance. As for Mozart, he found in Constanza nothing more than a substitute for happiness. Whether Bach, who had 13 children with a singer named Anna Magdalena, was really happy is unclear. Closer to our time, composers and singers have glorified lovers to the heavens: from Francis Lemarque to Georges Brassens, Charles Aznavour and Bernard Lavilliers, words and music find their best source of inspiration in love:

Lost Heart, Fishing for Hearts, Foolish Love, Loving Is Stronger Than Being Loved, The Sad Lovers, Love, A Cherry, Lovers on Public Benches, As Much Love as Flowers, The Bohemian, Love Is Wonderful, It's Always the First Time, The Man I Love, The Station-master in Love, Heart on a Tightrope, Hymn to Love, Thousands of Lost Kisses: it would take a whole encyclopedia of many volumes just to list the titles of love songs—without even considering the ones being written at this very moment. Love is truly "as old as the world." That's an understatement. . . .

Gala, whom we see here at the side of Salvador Dali
in Port Lligat in November of 1957, was formerly
involved with the poet Eluard before connecting
with the Spanish painter. In both cases, the woman
was an inspiration to the artist.

Ballad . . .

Tell me where, in what place
Are Flora the beautiful Roman,
Alcibiades, and Thaïs,
Who was her first cousin?
Where is Echo, who responds
To noise on river or pond,
And whose beauty was more than human?
But where are the snows of yesterday?

Where is wise Héloïs
For whom Pierre Exbaillart in Saint Denis
Was castrated and made a monk?
For his love he suffered this.
And where is the sovereign
Who ordered Buridan
Bound and tossed into the Seine?
But where are the snows of yesterday?

The queen white as a lily
Who sang with a siren's voice,
Big-footed Bertha, Beatrice, Alice,
Haremburgis who held Maine,
And Jeanne, the good girl from Lorraine
Whom the English burned at Rouen:
Where are they, where, sovereign Virgin?
But where are the snows of yesterday?

Georges Brassens at Bobino in 1969. Selection
from the *Ballad of Women from Time Past* by
François Villon, set to music by Brassens.

IMAGES OF LOVE

If one subject is common to many painters, it's love. As an excellent unifying theme, conjugal or platonic love, scenes of flirtation, and mythological figures have always inspired painters, from the most primitive to the most contemporary. Perhaps because allegorical love made portraying nudes possible, which was long forbidden in portraits and simple representations of people.

Beautiful finery and choice birds of prey for this lady and gentleman of the fifteenth century united by their love for the hunt.
Anonymous, Palazzo della Regione, Padua.

A pair of Venetian lovers in an enigmatic pose, painted by Bordone (1500–1571).
Art Gallery, Milan.

The Birth of Venus by Botticelli (1445–1510) still makes us dream.
Services Museum, Florence.

When you look closely at the Departure for Cythera, the famous tableau by Jean Antoine Watteau (1684–1721), you see that it represents more than a voyage: it depicts several gallant scenes.
The Louvre, Paris.

Visit to the Fiancée by Emile Loubon (1809–1863). Engagements were originally devised as a means for the lovers to get to know each other better.
Museum of Fine Arts, Marseilles.

Here is The Marriage of the Artist with Isabelle Brandt by Rubens (1577–1640)— evidently a marriage based on love.
Art Gallery, Munich.

The Trumpeter and the Servant Girl by Pieter Leermans (1655–1707).
Rennes Museum.

What tranquility in marriage behind the austerity of these two characters in the *Giovanni Arnolfini Marriage Portrait* by Van Eyck (ca. 1390–1441)! National Gallery, London.

Garden of Love in the Court of Philip the Good on the Occasion of his Chamberlain's Wedding (Sixteenth Century). Palace at Versailles.

Odalisque by Jean Baptiste Ange Tissier (1814–1876). National Museum of Arts from Africa and Oceania, Paris.

Here's what Jacques Serena wrote about *The Kiss* by Gustav Klimt (1862–1918): "Without even mentioning its celestial quality, the striking thing is the gold, and the sensation of ineffability it creates." Galleries of Austrian Art, Vienna.

The Kiss by Francesco Hayez (1791–1882) is filled with spirited love. Today's movies can't do any better with a topic like this one. Art Gallery, Milan.

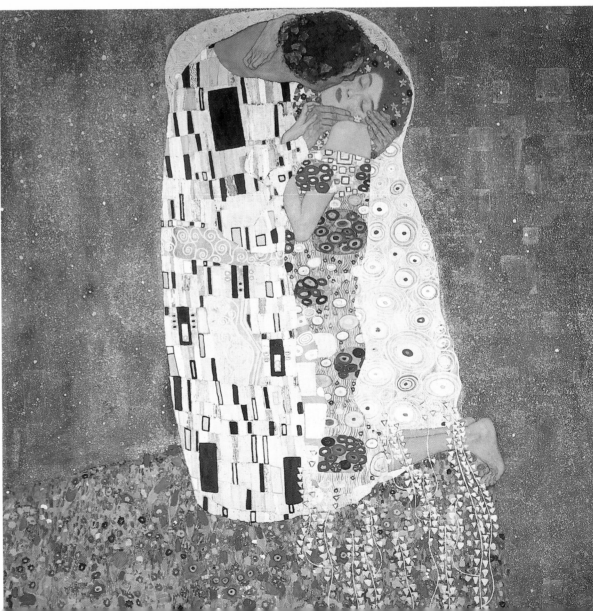

Daphnis and Chloë, represented here in statuary, exchange a sweet kiss. Their gestures of love evince perfect harmony. *Hôtel de Ville, Paris.*

Different Types of Love

Illustration for *The Sufferings of Young Werther*, the archetypal romantic work by Goethe (1749–1832), by Jean Baptiste Blaise Simonet (1742–1813).
National Library, Paris.

Speaking of love, and writing about love and lovers, is tantamount to writing down the history of all humanity since the beginning of the world. From Adam and Eve to the latest regal media marriages, from mythical loves to anonymous passions, lovers have kept the world turning. They have helped humans to enter this world, grow, create, and hope. Without love, the moving force behind our dreams, aspirations, and our very lives, we wouldn't be where we are today. With its impulses, its flights, its upsets, its troubles, its despair, plus its suffering and its drama, it has gone hand in hand with our history since the earliest times. Also, more than anything else, love sets our species apart from the rest of the animal kingdom, with its susceptibility to passion, voluptuousness, and transcendence of self.

Love has no age limit, and the same is true for lovers. Love stalks us for the duration of our existence. It's as moving to see it in an aged couple who carry on like lovebirds or rediscover it in everyday living, as to see it dawn fresh and innocent on the playgrounds of nursery schools.

"We are all engaged in the pursuit of a happiness that we rightly or wrongly think will come to us only through love."

From contented love to crimes of passion, from mystical ecstasy to a lavish wedding, we are all engaged in the pursuit of a happiness that we rightly or wrongly think will come to us only through love. Since the ways of the god of love are as impenetrable as those of the Christian God, this sentiment takes different forms. These forms are a source of continuous discussion. We have drawn up a list of some of them, but there are hundreds more, and more yet. . . .

—chaste love: Paul and Virginie, the disciples of Bernadin de Saint-Pierre, whose idyll unfolds on the luxuriant Maurice Island; Brigitte Fossey and Georges Poujouly in *Forbidden Games* by René Clément;

Georges Poujouly and Brigitte Fossey are the tender heroes of childhood love in René Clément's 1952 film *Forbidden Games*.

Only after 1769 (five years after the death of Madame de Pompadour) did the ravishing Madame du Barry (1743–1793) become Louis XV's favorite. Drawing by François Drouais (1727–1775).

The historic love between the Catholic monarchs Ferdinand II of Aragon and Isabella de Castile facilitated the unification of Spain in the fifteenth century.
Royal Chapel, Granada.

Othello and Desdemona by Theodore Chasseriau (1819–1856). While beset with jealousy, Othello, the Moorish general of Venice, murders Desdemona, who loves him.
Former Brame and Lorenceau collection.

"Historic loves: Mausolus and Artemis, Caesar and Cleopatra, Anthony and Cleopatra."

"Historic loves: Isabella of Castile and Ferdinand of Aragon; Sissi and François-Joseph of Austria."

—legendary love: Venus and Adonis: Adonis, loved by Venus, was killed by a wild boar and brought back to life by Zeus; Orpheus and Eurydice: in order to bring his beloved wife back to life, Orpheus went down to hell and confronted fearsome Cerberus; Solomon and the queen of Sheba; Philemon and Baucis: in their old age, they granted hospitality to Zeus, who out of gratitude later saved them from drowning and granted their wish never to be separated, transforming them into an oak and a lime tree; Ulysses and Penelope; Eros, god of love, and Psyche; Lancelot of the Lake and Guinevere: after being raised by Vivian, the fairy of the waters, the knight seduced Guinevere, King Arthur's wife, thereby making himself unworthy of finding the Holy Grail; Tristan and Isolde; The Cid and Chimene; Sleeping Beauty awoken by Prince Charming;

—historical loves: Mausolus and Artemis: upon the death of her husband, Artemis, queen of Halicarnassus, had a tomb constructed to honor the memory of her husband (that's the origin of the word *mausoleum*); Caesar and Cleopatra, Anthony and Cleopatra—after the suicide of Anthony, the queen of Egypt killed herself by getting bitten by an asp; Eloïse and Abélard; Isabella of Castile and Ferdinand of Aragon, rulers of Spain; Louis XIV and Mademoiselle de la Valliere, Louis XIV and Madame de Montespan, Louis XIV and Madame de Maintenon, whom he secretly married; Louis XV and Madame de Pompadour, Louis XV and Madame du Barry; Napoleon and Josephine de Beauharnais; Queen Victoria and Albert of Saxon-Cobourg-Gotha; Elizabeth de Wittelsbach, or Sissi as she was known to her good friends, and François-Joseph I of Austria; the Duke of Windsor and Wallis Simpson; John and Jackie Kennedy, a love that ended tragically;

The loves of Madame de Pompadour, who is shown in this painting by François Boucher (1703–1770), and of Louis XV had an impact on the king's policies.
Wallace Collection, London.

The great Spanish mystic Theresa of Avila (1515–1582) by Bernini (1598–1680).
Santa Maria della Vittoria, Roma.

Black Orpheus (Marcel Camus, 1959) adapts the ancient myth of Orpheus in love with Eurydice to cinema, giving it a modern context.

In 1683, Louis the Great secretly wed Madame de Maintenon, who stayed by him in his old age. Engraving by Moreau the Younger. Carnavalet Museum, Paris.

"Romantic loves: George Sand and Musset, George Sand and Chopin; Liszt and Marie d'Agoult . . ."

—platonic loves, for which the Princesse de Cleves, Madame de La Fayette's heroine, remains the model. Goethe also was hopelessly in love with Charlotte Buff (*The Sufferings of Young Werther* are an epistolary version of this passion);

—romantic loves: Madame de Staël and Benjamin Constant, exalted and melancholy souls; Lou Andreas-Salomé and Rilke; George Sand and Musset, George Sand and Chopin; Liszt and Marie d'Agoult before their breakup; Mimi and Rudolphe in *La Boheme*, Floria and Mario in *Tosca*, Cio-Cio San and an American officer in *Madame Butterfly* (three Puccini operas); D'Annunzio and Eleonora Duse; Apollinaire declaring his love for Louise de Coligny-Châtillon in *Shadow of My Love*, and Jean-Louis Trintignant and Anouk Aimée in the Lelouch film, *A Man and a Woman* (1966);

—mystical love: Theresa of Avila experienced ecstasy in her love of God;

—tragic love: Romeo and Juliet; Othello and Desdemona; Camille Claudel and Rodin;

—infernal love: Faust and Marguerite; Manon Lescaut and the knight des Grieux; Valmont and Madame de Mertueil as they circumvent the virtuous Madame de Tourvel in *Dangerous Liaisons*;

—schmaltzy love: the characters of Delly and Barbara Cartland, *The Two of Us*, the illustrated novel.

And so on; literature, history, and life are filled with true and imagined stories.

Emotion, fragility, and tenderness in the Claude Lelouch film, *A Man and a Woman* (1966), with Anouk Aimée and Jean-Louis Trintignant in the major roles.

The cover of the first issue of the magazine *The Two of Us*, published in May of 1947; its popularity ushers in the illustrated novel.

The idea of plastering one's love all over the town is a common folly.

Lovers' Follies

Love commonly gives rise to follies and extravagance in gifts in proportion or disproportion to the feelings of the afflicted person. That's why Czar Alexander III ordered from the goldsmith Fabergé a fabulous Easter egg for his Czarina Marina. At that time, it was a tradition in Russia to offer an egg to a loved person—a simple, brightly colored chicken's egg for modest people and eggs made of glass, precious wood, or porcelain for the well-heeled. However, never before that 1884 creation had an Easter egg reached the kind of price and splendor that earned Fabergé instant fame.

"Stars are susceptible to giving ruinous and eccentric gifts."

Closer to our time, we remember the diamond (the largest in the world next to the famous "Regent" housed in the Louvre) given by Richard Burton to Elizabeth Taylor as a token of his love; a slight folly, wouldn't you say? At any rate, stars have the privilege of doing such things when they want to. In the same vein, Zizi Jeanmaire received from her husband Roland Petit an ivory rose inlaid with a tear-shaped diamond. Let's not forget the famous car decorated with red hearts that Carole Lombard parked in front of Clark Gable's door nor the torrent of roses that Gunther Sachs had rain down on la Madrague, Brigitte Bardot's house.

As you can see, stars are susceptible to giving ruinous and eccentric gifts. They do not suffer from a lack of ideas or means to make come true the dreams that everyday couples can only imagine or experience vicariously by identifying with their favorite stars. There's no way they can give one another the Rolls Royce or the love nest on the French Riviera or in California that's common fare for celebrities. If you're not a star, sometimes all you can do is give your sweetheart a dozen roses from time to time.

Not all eccentricities are so costly: there was once a time when abducting one's sweetheart, or sending her a poem as a vow of faithfulness, was considered the height of romance. People used to carve two hearts onto the trunk of a tree, paint graffiti onto walls or picture windows, write, telephone—whatever shape it takes, it's still love. . . .

The Love Cypher, engraving by Nicolas de Launay (eighteenth century), after Fragonard.
National Library, Paris.

PEOPLE

PEOPLE

Love wouldn't be so fundamental and vital if it weren't so sought after, endowed with life, lived intensely, nourished, denied, rejected, and suffered by those who experience it profoundly. It would scarcely appear to be more than a vague notion, abstract and chimerical, an ideal devoid of substance, a fleeting desire. It's scarcely imagined that, with the exception of a few noteworthy cases, love has nothing to do with the needs of the flesh, numerous temptations, mundane problems, and daily suffering. People say that lovers are alone in the world. Even if the axiom is true for many anonymous couples, it's hardly the case for famous personalities. Their love affairs, which are displayed in broad daylight and are used as a means to bolster their prestige, have become nothing more than a set of external factors to pump them up but that, at the same time, tend to drag them down.

Artists have long celebrated the other half of the couple by painting their beloved, writing letters or poems, or composing music for her (most of the time, the man does these things). Abstract painting

hardly needs models anymore, and the laptop and the answering machine record laconic declarations of love; literature and movies show us in print or on the screen a violent reality where the definition of love—a strong affection for someone or something—is buried under a tide of vulgar words and intentions that oftentimes are equally base. Fortunately, people continue to write love songs. They're easier to listen to than a sonata, they come by radio, and as you drive you can sing along at the top of your lungs with Jacques Brel or Julien Clerc. So there's no reason to despair after all! Especially because it's all the same to love, which has alternately been exalted on high and dismissed as insignificant: love has survived through the ages, and it will be around for a lot longer.

People celebrate love in all kinds of ways, sometimes loving it—lovers in love with love—sometimes swearing that they'll never get caught by it again. Wrong again: they keep getting caught, forgetting when they sign a new lease all the rotten tricks that love has pulled on them. Here, by way of putting a face onto love, are some famous and some anonymous couples who at some point in their lives have played the role of lovers, for real or for make-believe.

From left to right:
The Sculptor Pygmalion in Love with His Statue and Begging Venus to Bring It to Life by Jean-Baptiste Regnault (1754–1829). Palace at Versailles.
Pierre and Marie Curie leave their laboratory for a little exercise (1896).
The Duke and Duchess of Windsor at a dog show in Deauville in 1959; time has passed, but happiness remains intact.
Elizabeth Taylor and Richard Burton in *The Sandpiper* (Vincente Minelli, 1965).
Joanne Woodward and Paul Newman: lovers in life as well as in film.

These contemporary lovers
support each other
as they stroll along.

Anonymous Couples

How do people "fall in love," and why does this expression that leads to love inevitably evoke the memory of the fall? It's equally noteworthy that one succumbs to passion, as if death were not far off, that one becomes madly in love as reason suddenly flies away under the intensity of the feeling. Thunderstruck also comes from the same vocabulary, at once evincing the absolute immediacy and the extreme violence of the impact.

At first, love is a mere spark. Whether the spark kindles into a blaze or a roaring fire is a matter of circumstances and will—or two wills—even if it seems at the time that the lovers have been divested of their free will. At first you live for yourself, and then the existence—the presence—of the other person changes everything. That person becomes irreplaceable, unique, the object of desire, phantasm, and reality all at once. You are transformed from *I* to *we*.

Loving means no longer belonging to yourself yet wanting the other person to belong to you totally and exclusively. Intoxication? Enchantment? Ecstasy? Folly? All that and yet none of it; for at that time and thereafter, you're incapable of analyzing your feelings. "He's handsome, everyone, he's nice, everyone!" The birds sing, and nature celebrates the fact. These premises of love are quite intense and more or less identified with one another. A lover is convinced he knows the other person even before possessing her. So marriage looks like the fatal end. People have long considered that love should be the result. Nowadays, it's neither the obvious nor the mandatory consequence. Rare are the young couples who, madly in love though they may be and filled with the best of intentions, believe today that marriage is "for the rest of their lives." Lady Chatterley's husband, paralyzed and impotent, asserts that "what counts is lifelong union, living together day after day and not merely jumping into bed a few times." This axiom is no longer valid: in the new century, lovers live for the moment. With joy and intensity, looking to

"Loving means no longer belonging to yourself yet wanting the other person to belong to you."

Little outward display and much sobriety in this wedding photo from 1900.

Sailors lined up for a parade turn around to watch one of their colleagues kiss his fiancée (1960).

Alone in front of the immensity of the ocean: love can often find contentment in such simple situations.

"Love that has become mere esteem and trust is no longer a hot commodity on the stock exchange of emotions."

the immediate future rather than further ahead. Time no longer has the same value: people no longer wait until they're "well situated" to get married. They love, they marry—or live together. Also, divorce is a lot more common than ever before. It's not that today's couples are more flighty or less desirous of a long-term commitment. However, the moral force of society is a lot less than it used to be. People prefer to separate rather than to waste a whole lifetime in a failed marriage.

Just the same, it's interesting to note that when you ask young people, marriage seems to be as much an intention to join one's life with that of a lover as it is a chance to have a party with friends. Sometimes the party turns out to be a success; sometimes it's a flop. You get over it as well as you can and as quickly as possible, the more so when another boy or girl strikes your fancy and makes you want to start all over again.

Captivating, appropriating, and keeping the other person—these are

Love hippie style: jeans and long hair, informal dress, body painting; in a word, "love and peace."

Today, people have cut their hair, but jeans are still around and so is happiness, just like in the sixties.

"To become one: that's the first and last goal of love."

the three phases that go into forming a couple, "a vibrant storm of energy, emotions, hopes, doubts, dreams, enthusiasm, and fear . . . a white-hot crucible where fusion forces collide with those that foster individuality. . . ."(1) To become one: that's the first and last goal of love. Desire is inseparable from feeling, and the more it is satisfied, the more it craves satisfaction. Before becoming passion, it is obsession. In *Lolita* by Nabokov, a crazy desire turns into the love of an adult for an adolescent. Eroticism is inseparable from love. Even when it's disguised, as it was in previous centuries, there's no denying it. Without it, a couple is no more than an association based on common interests, a shaky marriage, a solitude for two that quickly leads to adulterous temptations. Anonymous couples live their love with sincerity because they have no need to promote or overwork their image, much less to act out a role. They come and go, love each other, love each other less, and cease to love one another; they exchange promises and vows, insults, and even blows—all beyond the reach of the media. Secrets of the heart and secrets of the boudoir; sometimes secrets are a good thing. . . .

. . . Modern Poetry

She stands on my eyelids
And her hair mingles with mine.
She has the shape of my hands
And the color of my eyes,
She is swallowed up in my shadow
Like a stone against the sky.

Her eyes are always open
And she never lets me sleep.
Her daydreams
Make suns evaporate,
Make me laugh, cry, and laugh,
And talk with nothing to say.
Woman in Love Excerpt
from *Capital of Pain* by Paul Eluard

(1) *I love you. All About Passionate Love* by Francesco Alberoni, Paris, Pocket, 1999.

LOVE IN POSTCARDS

Love is not satisfied by its mere existence. You still have to know how to express it. Preferably with verve, style, and humor. Postcards are a good example of the tender or comical ways that lovers use to show their passion as soon as they have to leave the side of the object of their affection.

A 1910 lovers' tête-à-tête, where things aren't happening only above the table.

Par une fleur, l'amour peut tout traduire : L'espoir, le charme, et l'art de nous séduire !

There is a consuming desire to steal a little pleasure from time in the flower of our age. Like a flower, love is fragile . . . we must seize it before it's too late.

This couple from the twenties uses a horseshoe to express their desire to make their love last.

Are these two really going to end up in the water? Boats have always been a place for lovers to get together and pour forth their feelings. (This card is from 1900.)

This couple, from around 1910, who are dressed up to the nines, are drinking a toast to undying love.

Greeting card from the beginning of the century. A couple with a sled.

Postcard from around 1910; people enjoy sharing some secrets that exist only between lovers to create a little complicity. (The piano's there just for effect.)

Above: The writer Victor Hugo (1802–1885), whose companion and muse was the actress Julienne Gauvain, known as Juliette Drouet (1806–1883), **shown below**.

Muses of Painters, Writers, and Musicians

More sensitive than others to feminine beauty, artists have always celebrated womankind, whether they are in love with their model or just wish to idealize her.

In the twelfth century, Jaufré Rudel addressed the countess of Tripoli, his *Distant Princess*:

> *Desire draws my heart*
> *To that lady whom I love*
> *I have always sighed for her*
> *But there's no need to pity me,*
> *For joy is born of pain.*

"Give yourself over, oh divine Amaranth, submit to the will of love. . . ."

In the fourteenth century, Petrarch dedicated some despairing lines to Laura de Noves. Inaccessible because she was married, Laura died of the black plague in 1348. In 1336, Boccacio wrote *Love's Lover* for Marie d'Aquino, whom he met in the court of Robert d'Anjou; Marie was Robert's natural daughter. In the seventeenth century, Moliere wrote *Psyché* (evidently in collaboration with Corneille):

> *Let love awaken you tonight;*
> *Let yourself burn for my sighs:*
> *You sleep too much, you lovable wonder,*
> *For sleeping is not loving. . . .*
>
> *. . . Give yourself over, oh divine Amaranth,*
> *Submit to the will of Love;*
> *Love while you are charming,*
> *For time passes with no return.*

We know what type of role Juliette Drouet played with Victor Hugo starting in 1833. He dedicated a part of his work to her, including *Contemplations*. We know the revolution that countess Hanska produced in Balzac's life. We know the pathetic end of the stormy love between Alfred de Musset and George Sand in 1835.

In the twentieth century, Jacques Prévert celebrates *This Love*:

So violent

So fragile

So tender

So desperate...

...So happy

So joyous

And so pathetic...

...And so sure of itself...

Closer to us, Henri Pichette, a French writer born in 1924, imagines an erotic dialogue between *The Poet and the Lover*:

LOVER: I would be immortalized in you, like a gull, you would cut me with your wing.... I am yours!... You spill the azure in me. You punctuate my womb with burning yews. It's a celebration. I become porous. You ruffle my hair. I go with you. We slowly descend a purple staircase.... You carefully unfold voluptuousness, you detour my thirst, you prolong me, you chrysalis me and I am chosen again.... Then I dance, I dance, I dance; like a flame standing on the ocean with my eyelids closed.... Pleasure is sweetly painful....

POET: I print you

LOVER: I go before you

POET: I giddy you

LOVER: And you start me again

POET: I September, October, November, December you, and all the time that's needed.

At Montparnassus, at the start of the twentieth century, the surrealists sublimated the passion of woman, woman-child, or mediator. Nadja, the one he refuses to call by any name "to avoid offending her," had a considerable impact on the life of André Breton, who had some ambiguous relationships with her based more on intellectual seduction than on the enthusiasm he experienced successively for the woman of

Madame Hanska, the Polish wife of Balzac (1799–1850) (left), at first kept up an essentially epistolary relationship with the French writer.

From her liaison with the Hungarian composer and pianist Franz Liszt (1811–1886) (right), the French writer Marie de Flavigny, countess d'Agoult (1805–1876) (left), bore three children. One of her two daughters married Richard Wagner.

Elsa Triolet (1896–1970) was the wife of Louis Aragon (1897–1982), who professed a limitless love for her and, in 1942, composed a lyrical collection for her entitled *Elsa's Eyes*.

"Liszt became acquainted with Marie d'Agoult, who broke away from her mundane life, her friends, and . . . her husband."

Insane Love and the one in *Arcane 17*. As an epigraph to *Connected Vessels*, he wrote: "You will never be able to see that star as I used to see it; you don't understand: it's like the heart of a flower with no heart."

There are countless letters and passionate poems like this one from Aragon to his wife Elsa, plus countless declarations and marriage proposals. Countless too are the love novels that are still being published: *Autobiography of a Love* (Alexandre Jardin), *Can You Image Happy Love* (Pierre-Yves Bourdil), *From the Blues to Love* (Hanif Kureishi), *Love, Prozac, and Other Curiosities* (Lucia Extebarria), *The Loves of George Sand and Musset* (Bernadette Chovelon)—to name but a few of the recent ones. Love still brings in money.

Musicians, too, have always been inspired by muses. After being turned away by the father of Mademoiselle de Saint-Cricq, Liszt (at that time, he was merely an impecunious pianist) became acquainted with Marie d'Agoult, who, breaking away from her mundane life, her friends, and . . . her husband, had a decisive impact on his work—cerebral as well as sensual— and produced three children for him. Among them, Cosima, who was married to the great pianist and orchestra conductor Hans von Bülow, director of many of Wagner's works, didn't hesitate to leave him in 1863 to join up with the latter when his *Tannhäuser* fell flat. Prior to that, Wagner had composed, under the "regime" of Mathilda, wife of Otto Wesendonck, *The Rhinegold*, *The Walkyrie*, and part of the *Teratology*, when, in order to flee from scandal, he abandoned this last work to announce his despair in *Tristan*. The *Teratology* was finished much later, with Cosima.

Married in 1840 to Clara Wieck after numerous ups and downs, Schumann sang the happiness she gave him in Lieder with romantic titles: *Romances and Ballads*, *Love and the Life of a Woman*, *Loves of a Poet*. This period of happiness lasted ten years; after that, Schumann sank into a depression that only Clara's presence could soften. In 1782,

A German composer who became kapellmeister in Dresden, Richard Wagner (1813–1883) (right) left his country because of his revolutionary ideas. He found help notably with Franz Liszt, whose daughter Cosima (left) he married.

Mozart (1756–1791) married Constanza out of spite when her sister Aloysia rejected him; she brought him nothing but hassles and financial worries. Scarcely any happier, Berlioz managed the feat, after a relationship with a flirt who was cheating on him, of marrying an actress who spoiled his life. After leaving her, he took up with a second-rate singer who spoiled it even more.

Unlike his elders, Tchaikovski (1840–1893) was able to find in Nadejda von Meck, who had already helped Debussy, the comfort he needed after the failure of his marriage and the revelation of his homosexual tendencies. The only condition attached by the baroness to the encouragement she heaped onto the author of *The Nutcracker* and *Swan Lake*: we must never meet!

"Painters need the presence of their muse, a woman they love or at least admire."

This is exactly the opposite of what happened with the painters. They needed the presence of their muse, a woman they love or at least admire. In the Renaissance, Raphaël exalted feminine beauty in general and the Fornarina's in particular. A century later, Rembrandt owed his fame as a portraitist to Saskia Van Uylenburgh, whom he wed in 1634. At the same time, Rubens devoted several paintings to his young wife (*Helen Fourment, Helen and Her Son François*, 1635). Like Bonnard at the start of the twentieth century, whose wife inspired his *Backlit Nude*, Magritte responded to a questionnaire published in *Surrealist Revolution* in 1929 by writing: "All that I know about the hope that I put into love is that there is just one woman who can make it a reality." Dali glorified Gala, and Picasso the women who accompanied him throughout his life (*Portrait of Olga in an Armchair* for Olga Koklova, *Woman Crying* for Dora Maar, *Painter and His Model* when he met Jacqueline). Striking testimonials to love that have become veritable treasures and that museums and families fight over.

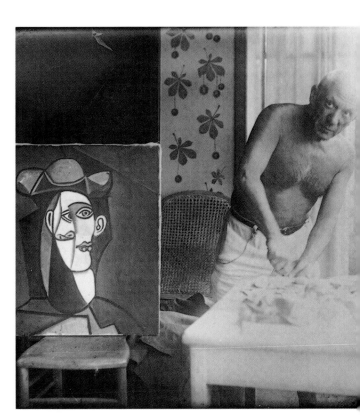

The metamorphosed feminine faces in the work of Pablo Picasso (1881–1973) are surely a reflection of his attraction to the women who accompanied him throughout his life.

Joanne Woodward and Paul Newman, photographed here in the fifties, have always been a well-adjusted couple who managed to evolve discreetly and stay together in the media-controlled world of the superstars.

In Real Life and the Movies: Star Couples

In contrast with couples whose identity is not widely known, famous pairs have often broken down the fragile barrier that separates their private and professional lives. A public eager for juicy stories and the media continually on the prowl for ways to whet that appetite are largely responsible as, in fact, are those personalities that are addicted to notoriety. Now star couples are found in all types of settings, in movies and the political sphere, in the fashion world, and in art and television. It's interesting to note that in this universe where appearances play a major role, the couples who flaunt themselves the most are frequently the ones with the slimmest chance of staying together. "To live happily, live privately": the old adage has lost none of its truth.

"The couples who flaunt themselves the most are frequently the ones who have the slimmest chance of staying together."

Joanne Woodward and Paul Newman have been married for more than forty years, and they are seen in Hollywood only when they absolutely can't avoid being there. Madeleine Renaud and Jean-Louis Barrault, who have now vanished from sight, used to cross the Champs-Elysées arm in arm without attracting the least attention. Giulietta Masina and Federico Fellini led a discreet life in Rome, far from the pomp of *La Dolce Vita*. In contrast, actors, singers, producers of all types, and models seeking publicity have no hesitation in using the couple as a promotional gimmick and as a way to look like lovers or to grant a photo, a report, or an interview.

"Certainly public appearances are proof that the couple exists for the benefit of, yet in opposition to, everyone else."

For some, public appearances are proof that the couple exists for the benefit of, yet in opposition to, everyone else, buffeted about, scorned, or ridiculed. The Clintons are the most recent and tragic example. Who will ever know if the Perons, who twice governed Argentina, managed to save a little spot of paradise for love behind all the power and the glory?

Love and power are rarely compatible; the second requires that the first efface itself to its demands. The Duke of Windsor understood that well

Yves Montand and Simone Signoret in 1953, when they were happy together.

Ingrid Bergman, Roberto Rosselini, and their children in Paris in June of 1954. A type of happiness. . . .

A passionate kiss between Humphrey Bogart and Lauren Bacall in *Dark Passage* (Delmer Daves, 1947).

John and Jackie Kennedy, photographed in May of 1962, show all the outward signs of matrimonial harmony. Reality, as we know, is something else entirely.

The "fairy-tale wedding" of Grace Kelly and Prince Rainier in April of 1956.

Elizabeth Taylor and Richard Burton shared an eventful passion of the kind seen only in the movies. Married and remarried, their public life was intimately mixed in with their private life. Here they are in the leading roles of *The Sandpiper* by Vincente Minelli in 1965.

Edith Piaf, beaming with Marcel Cerdan in March of 1948, has no inkling that one year later, her happiness will be interrupted by her partner's accidental disappearance.

when he abdicated rather than renounce the woman he loved, whose profile was not what was expected of a queen of England. (It was in fact quite a handsome profile, but of course here we are speaking neither of her face nor her silhouette.) Nor does Camilla Parker-Bowles have the qualities that are required in a sovereign, and it's obvious that every one of Prince Charles's public appearances with her causes protests. What a series of ruptures, deceptions, and forced smiles behind the clichéd couple who had the world on a string—John and Jackie Kennedy!

"What a series of ruptures, deceptions, and forced smiles behind the clichéd couple who had the world on a string!"

Then there are the "made-up" couples like Elizabeth Taylor and Richard Burton, who were not content to be married and remarried but who made films together, just like Yves Montand and Simone Signoret, and like Lauren Bacall and Humphrey Bogart. They didn't always have smooth sailing. What these sacred monsters did have in common, though, was a resistance to adversity that creates bonds that are stronger than fleeting and flamboyant passions.

Others, in contrast, have an obligation to show themselves, whether by predilection or by contract. They have to be seen together, young,

Jane Birkin and Serge Gainsbourg consent to sign a few autographs for their fans at Caesars in 1979.

Facing: Bogart and Bacall, the leading couple in *The Big Sleep* (1946); they had undeniable class both in real life and in the movies.

CINEMA
(excerpts)

LB = Lauren Bacall
HB = Humphrey Bogart

HB: Would you like to do something for me? Turn around for me. Turn. Don't you see anything?
LB: No. No connection. Not yet. (Embrace) I like it. Except the beard. Why don't you shave? We could try again.

The Port of Pain (1944–1945) by Howard Hawks.

LB: You like to play practical jokes, don't you? Why did you stop me?
HB: Because your father hired me, or because a Sternwood caught my eye.
LB: I prefer the second version.

The Big Sleep (1946) by Howard Hawks.

beautiful, smiling—but please check your weapons at the door. Stars of the small and big screen, rock stars, singers, and athletes—their appearances are often timed to coincide with the debut of a film, an album, or a performance. Attacks on private lives have led to some resounding legal cases and some damage awards sufficient to give pause to a number of hard-core paparazzi.

In addition to these lovers who put themselves on display whenever or wherever it serves their purposes, there are those who jealously or even pathologically protect their private lives. Americans are less fussy about this than the French, even if from time to time one of them has a fit and grapples with a photographer or a journalist whose curiosity rubs him or her the wrong way. Admittedly, some journalists in search of a scoop or a scandalous article cross the threshold to forbidden topics that a part of the reading public wants.

The definition of happiness clearly differs according to whether or not you're in the foreground. That the footlights are compatible with love is not a foregone conclusion.

COUPLES IN THE MOVIES

Of course, daily life has very little to do with the type of life the movies like to depict. However, that doesn't keep even the least romantic among us from having dreamed at one time or another of being in the arms of a Clark Gable, a Paul Newman, a Jean Gabin, or a Leonardo di Caprio, an Elizabeth Taylor, a Michelle Pfeiffer, or a Kate Winslet.

In *Gone with the Wind* (Victor Fleming, 1939), Rhett Butler (Clark Gable) has to expend a lot of effort to conquer Scarlett O'Hara (Vivian Leigh).

The love between Rose (Kate Winslet) and Jack (Leonardo di Caprio) breaks through social barriers: he breathes the air of freedom in *Titanic* (James Cameron, 1998).

James Mason and Sue Lyon in Stanley Kubrick's 1962 film *Lolita*. Adapted from the erotic novel by Nabokov, this misunderstood film leaves the viewer wishing for a little more.

John Cassavetes and Gena Rowlands in *The Tempest* (Paul Mazursky, 1982), embracing with a glass of champagne: a great game.

In *The Human Beast* (Jean Renoir, 1938, based on a work by writer Emile Zola), Jean Gabin falls in love with the wife of a murderer: behind the darkness of the film, a great love story develops.

Although abandoned by her husband (Paul Newman) at the start of the film *Cat on a Hot Tin Roof* (Richard Brooks, 1958), Maggie (Elizabeth Taylor) ends up having him give her the child she desperately wants.

Interesting picture by Epinal representing *The Tree of Love*.

"Hey, this is amazing! This morning I tied this lace into a square knot, and now it's in a bow!" Engraving by Paul Gavarni.

Lover hiding in a closet, a classic vaudeville scene from a genre that was popular at the start of the twentieth century.

Scandalous Love

Scandalous love defies the conventions of the time and fashionable morality or pushes its own logic to so-called crimes of passion. With the passage of time, these loves, which are the talk of the town, come to be regarded as examples, as if their marginality and their very excesses give them an aura of the uncommon.

Must we examine whether a vindictive spirit, or jealousy carried to a violent outbreak, is a proof of love? No, not according to criminologists and psychiatrists. It's a childish fear of being abandoned that impels certain people to murder the object of their passion. A crime of passion doesn't reflect in any way the intensity or the quality of love but, rather, some inadequacies in the constitution of the perpetrator.

Gaston Calmette, above, director of *le Figaro*; he was murdered by Madame Caillaux, below, on March 16, 1914.

A grotesque mask located at Puy; it symbolizes the perennial attitude of the deceived husband with its inscription: "My, how nicely horns fit on a forehead like mine."

Sometimes love turns violent. Here Anthony Quinn takes a roundhouse slap from his partner Shelley Winters in *Flap* (Jerry Adler, 1970). Theirs is a type of mean-spirited love.

The Poet and His Double

If you are a man. Admit it.
My angel of ceruse, your beauty
Captured on film by an
Explosion of magnesium.

Jean Cocteau
Heurtebise the Angel

Jean Cocteau and Jean Marais: years of artistic collaboration. One offered the other his best roles, the second one breathed life into them and transformed them.

"The excesses borne of passion can be inspiring and imaginative."

Criminal considerations aside, what are we to think of an excess of love that brings someone to exhume the body of a deceased loved one? In *Gil Blas* (1884), Guy de Maupassant reports that a young and brilliant lawyer in Béziers was discovered in a cemetery digging up the coffin of his beloved girlfriend, who had died at the age of twenty. All he could say in his defense was, "I loved her. I loved her, not with a sensual love, not with a simple tenderness of heart and soul, but with an absolute love, complete and boundless." He was acquitted.

Among loves that caused a scandal—it's hard to imagine it nowadays—homosexual liaisons have played a significant part, at least throughout the nineteenth and twentieth centuries when bourgeois morality has been unable to accept idylls between men or between women. Except perhaps in the case of artists, because they are already considered to be marginal by proper society. Even when they were as famous as Proust or Colette.

The media echo epic and passionate news items by attracting the readers' or the audience's attention to them so they can declare victory or scandal. We all remember the accident on August 31, 1997, that took the life of Princess Diana at age thirty-six and her friend, the Egyptian billionaire Dodi al-Fayed, age forty-two. This tragic fate had major repercussions in the media world and throughout the world in general. Ever since, Parisians and tourists have been coming to pay homage to the couple and leave flowers at the site of the accident.

Death in Venice
(Luchino Visconti, 1971):
a magnificent film, based
on the novella by Thomas
Mann, who broaches the
subject of homosexuality
with modesty and a
great artistic sense.

*Bonnie and
Clyde* (Arthur
Penn, 1966).
A movie
about two
bandits who
terrorized
American
society
during the
depression of
the 1930s.

Great Women Lovers

 rom Cleopatra to Lucrecia Borgia, great lovers for all eternity, seductresses have punctuated history. Diane de Poitiers exercised a real influence on Henry II, her junior by 19 years. Henry IV never got over the disappearance of Gabrielle d'Estrées, whom he was about to marry and who had given him three natural, legitimized children. In the case of Madame Pompadour, it's said that in order to seduce her royal lover (Louis XV), she would prepare broths using egg yolks, truffles, grated chocolate, and celery. When Catherine the Great was asked to produce an heir to the Russian throne, she had caviar delivered for dinner, along with the best built of her army officers.

"Seductresses have punctuated history."

Marguerite de Valois (1553–1615), better known by the name of Queen Margot, was reputed to devour men. It's said that Josephine de Beauharnais didn't observe absolute fidelity to a husband often absent in the Napoleonic Wars. Besides Musset and Chopin, George Sand had a husband and quite a few children without ever ceasing to assert that we must "inaugurate and sanctify love, lost and profaned in the world."

With regard to Mata Hari, the Dutch dancer and adventurer (1876–1917), how are we to distinguish between pleasure and duty in her numerous adventures? Marlene Dietrich has seduced generations of men with *Blue Angel* (1930) . . . along with Jean Gabin.

How about Marilyn Monroe (1926–1962)? If she was never fully happy, she at least tried valiantly, piling up marriages and affairs, none of which succeeded in bringing her happiness. Brigitte Bardot was able to escape that fate; she must be a little more adept at life.

On the marriage hit parade, Elizabeth Taylor (seven marriages) follows in the footsteps of Lana Turner (eight marriages in less than 30 years) and beats Zsa-Zsa Gabor (with just five).

The passions of all these women sparkle with radiance and make many women envious, but they seldom amount to any more than a flash in the pan.

The life and work of George Sand (1804–1876) evolved at the behest of her passions. Among her numerous lovers were Frederic Chopin and Alfred de Musset.

She used to sing that her audience was her "most beautiful love story." Barbara, "the lady in black" who disappeared in 1997, was a woman who loved her audience and showed it.

. . .Cleopatra, Femme Fatale

In the first century B.C., Anthony and Cleopatra, in love with one another, made up an indivisible couple that was nonetheless highly criticized at the time. It was a union between a high-ranking Roman and a "barbarian." Here's an excerpt from a contemporary work about Cleopatra. The scene is set in Actium at the time of the confrontation between Octavius and Anthony: "Anthony, with his barbaric strength and his arms of all kinds . . . carries Egypt and the powers of the East with him, . . . and he is followed by an Egyptian wife (what an abomination!). . . . The queen leads her troops with her sistrum* and can't yet see the two snakes that are behind her."

Excerpt from *The Aeneid* by Virgil, based on the translation by Maurice Rat.

*Ironic use of a word designating a religious instrument. Allusion to the queen's superstition.

Picture of a tragic fate and a lonely life. Marilyn Monroe, photographed in the 1950s, hugs a bronze statue.

AUG.ST GARNEREY

PLACES

PLACES

In the fifties, Georges Brassens had a big hit with his song *Lovers on Public Benches*. At that time, it was still considered bad manners to intertwine on benches or anywhere else in public. However, things have changed today, at least in many places. It can also be said that there are no more places set aside for kissing and that lovers feel at home no matter where they are, as if they were all alone in the world. Just the same, every budding couple dreams of visiting certain places hand in hand. Paris, Venice, Bruges, Prague, Amsterdam, Vienna, Seville . . . all seem like cities so appropriate for fostering love that lovers almost tend to forget that people live there, work, die, and . . . love, too. Just like everywhere else.

It's clear that water plays a major role in the status acquired by places for lovers. Venice and Bruges are cities built on or around water. The

Little Mermaid of Copenhagen is witness to strolling couples from all around the world. Lakes Maggiore and de Garde promote romance Italian-style, just like love temples erected in the middle of bodies of water, the flowered canals of Amsterdam, and the banks of the Seine in Paris.

Likewise boats, whether a simple canoe, a sightseeing boat, or a passenger ship—not all of them end up as tragically as the *Titanic*—are preferred places for some who cast off and sail happily for a few hours or several weeks. Water reflects an intertwined couple, the nimbus of a halo or a reflection that blurs the edges of reality and transforms it into a dream that's at once impalpable yet accessible. Famous or unknown, even intimate, lovers' retreats are infinite in number and as varied as love itself. From the Grand Canal to a hotel room, from the Malmaison Château to a recessed doorway. However, in some high-class places, love proclaims loudly and from on high its right to exist.

From left to right:
A love temple in the gardens at Versailles.
A siesta in the sun aboard a Venetian gondola.
Lovers embracing on the riverbanks in Paris (1958).
Dance at the *Moulin de la Galette* at Montmartre by Auguste Renoir (1841–1919).
D'Orsay Museum.
King Fahd's ocean liner carries its passengers on a dream cruise and an escape.
The island of Santa Lucia in the Antilles, under parasols and palm trees.

Around the World: Great Classics

Love wavers between dreams and myths, and obvious facts and reality. It aspires to experience them in fantastic places that more than anything allow it to take on a concrete form. While the most pedestrian of these places can be transformed into an unexpected and heavenly haven, others have universal appeal.

The winner among all these places, in the opinion of many people, is of course Venice—an admirable dream of stone and water, an inimitable model dear to lovers' hearts, with its Grand Canal where the gondolas glide along, its sumptuous palaces from another era, its tiny bridges, its alleyways

intersected by staircases discolored with age, its churches decorated by the greatest painters, its intimate and peaceful squares, its lazy cats, its statues, its cafés, the pigeons of Saint Mark's square, its inhabitants and hotels that celebrate it at every possible opportunity. The Danieli is still murmuring about the tumultuous love between Alfred de Musset and George Sand, and the Lido about the moving but hopeless passion of an aging man that Thomas Mann transformed in *Death in Venice*.

Nicknamed "The Venice of the North," Bruges likewise offers lovers canals, a lake of love, paved alleys, and flowering gardens. In Venice, where the shadow of Sissi still glides along, carriages drawn by white horses carry

Above:
Sunset on Venice, prelude to the nocturnal gondola rides that lovers are fond of.
Right:
The Bridge of Sighs attracts many lovers, but it gets its name from the convicts who were formerly led over it from prison to the torture chamber.

Gliding along silently in a gondola on the canals is an unforgettable moment in a visit to Venice.

At night, Venice is an enchanting place made for love; light adds to the magic of the place.

In Vienna, people still dream in front of the Château de Schönbrunn, which harbored the love between Elizabeth—the legendary Sissi—and her husband François-Joseph I, emperor of Austria from 1848 to 1916.

In Paris, people appreciate the splendors of the city from a sightseeing boat. Notre Dame "religiously" watches over lovers on the riverside promenades.

lovers on the traditional promenade on the Ring. Even if there are hardly any more balls given at the Château de Schönbrunn, there isn't a woman anywhere who hasn't fantasized at the sound of a Viennese waltz about dancing with the man of her dreams, if not the man of her life.

Some other European cities are just as welcoming to people who vow to love each other forever. In Prague, people kiss in front of the statue of the poet Mácha, who wrote an "Ode to Passion." In Copenhagen, people shed a tear as they pass in front of the Little Mermaid from Andersen's fairy tales, who died from loving her handsome prince too much.

Despite its northern mists, in Seville, you can set aside the mortification of holy week to admire the beautiful architecture. This destination is nearly mandatory for young married Spaniards, even if marriage has lost a bit of its force as a deterrent, there as everywhere. However, the gardens have retained the same seductive and dreamy power.

At the other end of the world, Niagara Falls, located half in the United States and half in Canada, is witness to a steady stream of honeymooning couples. The twin cities of Niagara Falls are known as the "Honeymoon Cities," and one of the falls is named "Bridal Falls." It's a complete program. . . .

"In Prague, people kiss in front of the statue of the poet Mácha, who wrote an 'Ode to Passion.'"

Above: Ever since 1913, the Little Mermaid of Copenhagen, gazing seaward, reminds passersby of the moving tale by Andersen. Lovers send her a melancholy thought.

Right: Since the start of the twentieth century, the Côte d'Azur has been the refuge of rich lovers who seek a sumptuous setting for their idylls.

Another part of the world celebrates the cult of love. The Taj Mahal is the palace constructed by the Emperor Shah Djahan to honor the "chosen one of the palace," his favorite wife from among the many that his Moslem religion allowed him and who died while giving birth to his fourteenth child.

While insane with grief, the emperor brought together architects from around the globe to construct at Agra, in the north of India, this luxurious mausoleum of white marble. Construction lasted from 1630 to 1653. When the emperor didn't have enough time to erect a similar monument in black marble, he was buried next to the wife he had loved so much.

Left:
The impressive falls at Niagara, separating Canada from the United States, are an ideal place for lovers who want to engrave their honeymoon onto their memory.

Right:
The heart of the old city of Bruges makes a complete set with its belfry and Rosary Dock—both for lovers, on account of this incredibly romantic setting, and art lovers who likewise have a field day.

Right: Saint Bartholomew—an island in Guadeloupe—once a paradise for billionaires, with its beaches that are the most beautiful of the Caribbean, is now open to lovers from around the world. People in the know call it Saint Bart.

Go over the bridge into Venice and meet at the Danieli Hotel, which has been host to many well-known love affairs.

"The islands are an ideal refuge for people who are in love."

In Rajastan, in the north of India, a number of palaces that formerly belonged to maharajahs have been remodeled into hotels that offer (especially at Jaipur, the pink city) specially equipped "honeymoon rooms." Paris remains a special place for lovers from all over. A City of Light that kindles sparks in the eyes of lovers who discover it from the Eiffel Tower or Montparnasse Tower, a sightseeing boat, or even a bus. There young and old couples celebrate real or pretended marriages, anniversaries of weddings and meetings, and emerging or well-established relationships. Paris offers many and varied kinds of pleasure, from the cabarets of Pigalle (some of which are not recommended for young, blushing brides, if such a thing still exists) to the romantic Montsouris Park, passing by Vosges Square and the Ritz bar. But you can't count on Paris alone. The Côte d'Azur isn't just for billionaires anymore. In Biarritz, the Love Chamber keeps boys and girls fantasizing. Islands are obviously ideal refuges for lovers.

Far from the world, they believe, and free to join it again when *they*, and no one else, decide. With its turquoise lagoons, Maurice Island (the fictitious homeland of Paul and Virginie), Malta, Saint Martin, and Saint Bartholomew are currently riding a wave of success. White sand, palm trees, and lush vegetation foster incipient relationships, and scents and spicy foods invite eroticism.

The famous Orient Express is also a source of eroticism and love. It leaves from the East Station in Paris (this is the least romantic part of the trip) and passes through Austrian Tyrolia and Innsbruck before arriving at Venice in the wee hours of the morning. It's expensive, but the Art Nouveau decor justifies the sacrifice, and you can still record

Like all cities punctuated by canals, Amsterdam is a favorite among lovers who are sensitive to the fairy-tale atmosphere that its waterways exude.

Below:
Saint John's Bay in the Antilles invites lovers to lounge on the beach as they toast in the sun.

The magnificent Square of Spain in Seville enthralls lovers who are fond of Arabic and baroque arts.

In Tyrolia, the city of Innsbruck, located close to ski areas, is an ideal winter honeymoon destination.

Left: The Isle of Capri in the Gulf of Naples offers lovers steep shores and grottos that are fun to explore.

this trip from Paris to Venice as something special on wedding lists. It's worthy of note that trips figure prominently on lovers' wish lists, even ahead of silver and tea services. The Italian lake region is still a favorite destination for couples in search of romance. At the foot of the Dolomites, Lake Guardia recalls Gabriele D'Annunzio, who had a luxurious house built there. Stresa the Magnificent and the Borromean Islands still work the same magic on young and not-so-young married couples who dream in front of the hanging gardens collapsing under quantities of flowers. When going as far as Como, they lounge in Bellagio ("How can one describe this emotion? You have to be in love and unhappy," Stendhal wrote about this village where the shades of Sissi, a tireless traveler, and Liszt still hover) and take in at least a cup of tea, if not a whole night, in the Villa d'Este, a former residence of cardinals and kings who had good taste and plenty of money. For those who prefer luxury to nostalgia, the obvious choice is Capri and its infallibly azure sea. However, the most unusual, the shortest, and one of the least expensive honeymoon trips is one taken on board a hot-air balloon. A flight over Burgundy and the Loire Valley, plus dinner and a night's lodging—that's material for the memory of a lifetime.

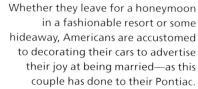

Whether they leave for a honeymoon in a fashionable resort or some hideaway, Americans are accustomed to decorating their cars to advertise their joy at being married—as this couple has done to their Pontiac.

Couple in a boat around 1900.

The Hotel Crillon in Paris is famous for its outstanding suites. Here we see a small living room that opens onto an outdoor terrace. The champagne is ready, and the easy chairs open their arms to us: this is an omen for a good stay.

Hideaways

Secrecy is one ingredient of love. In each person's eyes, the mystery of the other is entire, at least for a while, before the feeling solidifies or vanishes abruptly, just as unexpectedly as the thunderbolt that caused it.

"This stage of secrecy is essential to the formation of the couple."

This stage of secrecy is essential to the formation of the couple. It naturally leads to meetings and get-togethers. This is what people used to call *getting to know each other*, which is another stage that people foster and prolong through plans for the future—and that they scrap entirely if the relationship lasts for only a couple of days or is nothing but a one-night stand. In such situations, lovers forget the exterior—family, friends, relations of any kind—to withdraw with and into the object of their love. They need solitude, or at least intimacy. This is not the heat of pairing, but it's beyond mere indifference, hostility, and approval of people around them. They're not yet at the point of showing themselves in broad daylight. They savor one another heart

In order to be happy, going to famous or fashionable places is not necessary. Any beach or dune will do for couples in love.

The Grand Canal at Versailles also harbors lovers. Here they sleep in the sun.

Above: The bar in the Danieli Hotel offers its customers warmth and comfort. It was formerly one of the most luxurious palaces in Venice.

Right: An interior view of a temple in the gardens of the royal park at Versailles; love strings its bow in the club of Hercules.

Left: Love always triumphs in the paintings of Jean Cotelle (a painter under Louis XIV). In front of three fountains at Versailles, cherubs surround young girls wearing crowns.

and body, they laugh and live as a pair. The beginnings of passion are a flight into the self; the other person becomes a part of you and a rejection of the exterior world.

Lovers need to reserve some intimate places for themselves, usually unknown to others. They may be symbolic like a public bench, a temple of love, or the shore of a lake; we recall the one at Bourget that Lamartine wrote about. . . .

> *Oh time, suspend your flight*
> *And your sweet hours*
> *Suspend your course*
> *Let me savor the fleeting delight*
> *Of the sweetest of our days.*

It may also be as neutral as a car or a hotel bed ("They arrived, holding hands, two wondrous cherubs," sang Edith Piaf). Though we may look like cherubs, even for an instant, no place is henceforth impersonal when you make love in it for the first time.

Young Love's Green Pastures

Embrace in a Hayfield by Eugene Leon Labitte (1858–1937).

"Your first love changes you forever; it stays eternally with and within you."

I t starts like a nursery rhyme: you're four, five, or six years old and you're in love. Joys and troubles are important at that age. Later on, love is lived with intensity, with the most absolute urgency, incurable irresolution, unadulterated happiness, and the darkest adversity. Nothing is easy in adolescence.

Young love's green pastures are not always as green as they seem. As you grow up, it passes through all the hues of the rainbow.

Just the same, your first love changes you forever; it stays eternally with you and within you. Love in childhood and adolescence takes on a different hue, and that's when you begin to look for places to shelter it. Nowadays, a number of adolescents bring a boyfriend or girlfriend home, and the parents look the other way if that person spends the night in their house. Let's not forget that for some time now, IDs have not been required at motels (some countries still require them) and that the age of majority is set at eighteen.

So in order to love one another, couples had to connive, find a comfortable haystack, or find a gazebo at the end of the garden in the country, or a grotto or a beach suggested by a sympathetic friend, or for those who live in the city, a cul-de-sac or a little-used corridor in a building. Since things are always more appealing if we have to work for them rather than having them served to us on a silver platter, perhaps the time when people had to search out places to live their love far from the gaze of others was a guarantee that the love would last for a long time, or even forever.

If you can rely on statistics and on memory, that may be true. Nothing can beat the story my grandfather used to tell about the first time he wooed my grandmother at the bend of a small road. . . .

Shhh! . . . Those are family secrets. Ernest and Bernardine wouldn't have wanted me to broadcast that to everybody!

Young lovers flirting as they leave school. Changeable adolescent love sometimes creates great memories.

80

Between classes and at the end of the day there's a little free time; a boy whispers into his girlfriend's ear.

When love holds no more
secrets, lovers walk together in
the streets, like these partners
under a streetlight.

places

Public Places

Once lovers are sure that their feeling is reciprocal, they feel free to come out in broad daylight. You can't stay hidden forever. They renew with their surroundings, the friends they've neglected for a while, and the family to whom they'll sooner or later have to introduce the "chosen one." That's the time when they can walk hand in hand and kiss shamelessly on café terraces. They now have the courage to display their love to everyone. It's a crucial step that turns a secret happiness into good fortune known to the general public. Often, it's a prelude to a transformation from a duo of lovers to a couple that's established or at least on the way to becoming so.

Is a public place the opposite of a private and intimate place? Certainly not, at least as far as love is concerned. It's rather the logical consequence, its complement. After being cut off from the world, you return to it. You come back. You work together, you go for a walk, you go out, you look for an apartment. You exchange some lover's talk. When you're done whispering, you speak loudly and clearly. We have all met couples whose love and affection are moving . . . or annoying. It's not easy to accept happiness in others. We may even be a little

jealous of them—that blonde with a perfect figure, that boy who's the spitting image of Tom Cruise, who fixes his gaze onto her—when they lift their heads toward the street or the park or kiss each other on the lips right on the terrace of a café. The concept of modesty has changed quite a bit. Not so long ago, although it seems long ago, in a couple of European countries whose initials are Italy and Spain, the police had to bring some lovers back to order when they got carried away by their tempestuous passions. Since modesty is not the straitjacket it once was, lovers intertwine and kiss in public. They fight or make up. Passersby, and even the whole neighborhood, are called as witnesses.

As a sign of the times. Girls no longer hesitate to proposition boys whom they think are too timid. Of course, people no longer carve their

The view of the Eiffel
Tower from Trocadero is
a reward for many
strolling lovers.

It's great to bask in the sun together on the Pont des Arts in Paris next door to the Louvre!

Above: People take time for enjoyment in this outdoor café in Paris during the thirties, in an atmosphere seasoned by the Popular Front and paid holidays.

Lovers all around the world seem to appreciate more than anyone else the usefulness of public benches in showing their feelings. Here, in Armenia, despite the snow, a kiss warms bodies and hearts.

Above: Ever since the existentialists put Saint-Germain-des-Prés on the map, the café Flore in Paris has become one of the best places to be seen. That's no obstacle to lovers who choose to woo each other there.

Below: The banks of the Seine in Paris, from the Pont-Neuf to the Ile Saint-Louis, are a paradise for romantic souls in search of solitude.

name alongside their lover's into a tree trunk. In Paris, though, they continue to visit the Sacré-Coeur Basilica, the Eiffel Tower, and the Grévin Museum, to walk down the Champs-Elysées, and to pay a visit to the trendy bars.

From a sightseeing boat, you discover a city unlike any other. You drink a glass on the terrace of the Deux Magots or the Flore as you ponder the existentialists. You go shopping on Montaigne Avenue or, more inexpensively, in the department stores and little shops in les Halles. You catch your breath in the Luxemburg Gardens or Vosges Square. In short, you loiter around Paris, and that's happiness in itself.

"From a sightseeing boat you discover a city unlike any other."

Lovers like to discover other magical places, too, from Versailles to Monte Carlo, passing through Alsace and Courchevel, the Béarn, and Gascony. However, even though France is a premiere destination for tourists, it doesn't have a monopoly on places for people to linger. Even though lovers live to travel and discover, they don't always need famous places to create memories: a public bench, a square, the subway, or a doorway is all they need. Instead of dining at the Grand Véfour or at

Above: In England, too, people take shelter in entryways as they embrace.
Right: The Sacré-Coeur Basilica in Montmartre is a pleasant setting for lovers in Paris.

"Lovers no longer need to hide to be in love."

Maxim's, as in the Belle Epoque, they now kiss between bites of hamburger, perched on stools in fast-food joints, a motorcycle helmet in one hand and a cigarette in the other. "Lovers are alone in the world," and the world should always treat them kindly. If you only knew how lovers make sport of it! . . . They no longer need to hide to be in love, and they no longer need the blessing of the mayor or the priest. As for parental approval, desirable though it may be, they can easily get by without it. They just want to be with each other, look at each other, touch each other, love one another, and reassure one another. Where they do so matters little.

The world is not so frightening. Most of the time, they are sure of themselves and their feelings. In-love-forever is a play that they willingly act out in public.

A well-hidden lens looks down on this couple on a public bench on the banks of the Seine (around 1946).

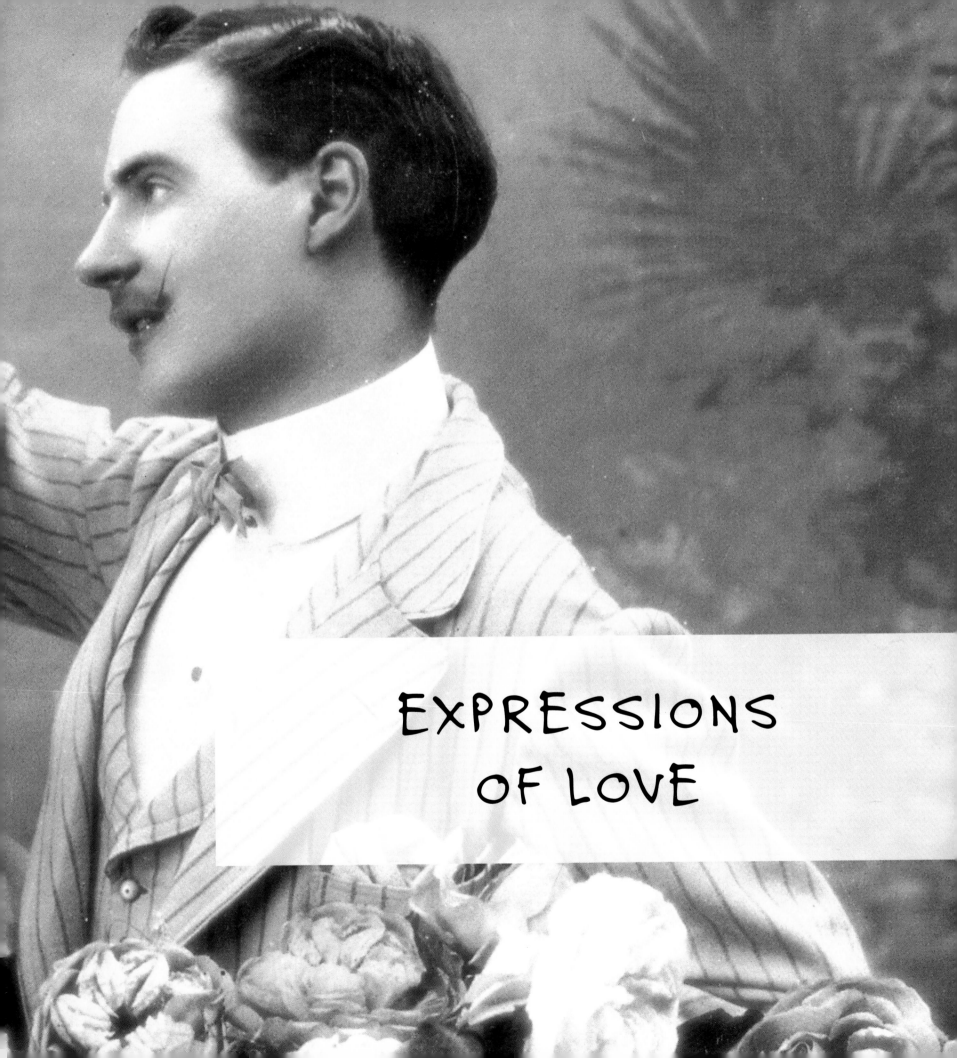

EXPRESSIONS
OF LOVE

EXPRESSIONS OF LOVE

ove can live and find true affirmation only if it's given enough room to express itself. Not long ago, a meaningful look, or a squeeze, or a kiss on the hand was enough to express the ardor of one's flame. Nowadays we're a good deal more demonstrative and more exacting in regard to impulses of the heart and body. The most fearful and clumsy among us could scarcely get by without hugs and kisses. Passionate ones. Long periods of abstinence are no longer appropriate in our western value system. Sensual pleasure, starting with the first mutterings of passion, has gained acceptance over the past two or three decades. From that point on, words to express it, and gestures for doing it, are the order of the day.

Not every love hits like a thunderbolt. It doesn't fall to everyone to become a victim or a lucky beneficiary of the storm that provokes psychological and sensory reactions that can include trembling, a feeling of cold followed by a sensation of extreme heat, and eruptions of verbal or body language.

Other types of love are more sedate, and even reasoned or induced. Expressions vary as a consequence: exuberant or affected, rare or frequent, out of place or touching in the eyes of observers, or delicious and savory to the recipient.

If we had to choose a single symbol of love, the kiss surely would garner all the votes. There's a reason it's seen as a prelude to making love, to uniting with and melting into a partner. Love is crazy about all types of expression, and every one of them is a reason for lovers to show their feelings. The wildest lovers' terms, love notes, phone messages, symbolic gifts . . . imagination seems to have no limits for lovers of a moment or an eternity. Not even Valentine's Day is capable of crystallizing all the movements of the heart.

Nowadays, since formality and the weight of social conventions are less than in the past, marriage is no longer an end in itself. It's only the official and concrete form of a shared love, the confirmed expression of a common will to go to the end of the line together and a great reason to celebrate. Love now takes the most diverse and contradictory forms. People get married or not, but in any case, it's still a union for better or for worse.

From left to right:
Movie couple embracing in a recent remake of *The Wings of a Dove* (Iain Softley, 1997). It doesn't get any better for bashful lovers!
Variations on postcard lovers from before 1914.
The language of kisses: postcard in the style of the 1920s.
The future emperor of Japan and his wife appear here in western dress on the occasion of their marriage in 1993.
English Valentine, or how to mend a broken heart with adhesive tape.
An American in Paris (Vincente Minnelli, 1951) with Gene Kelly and Leslie Caron.

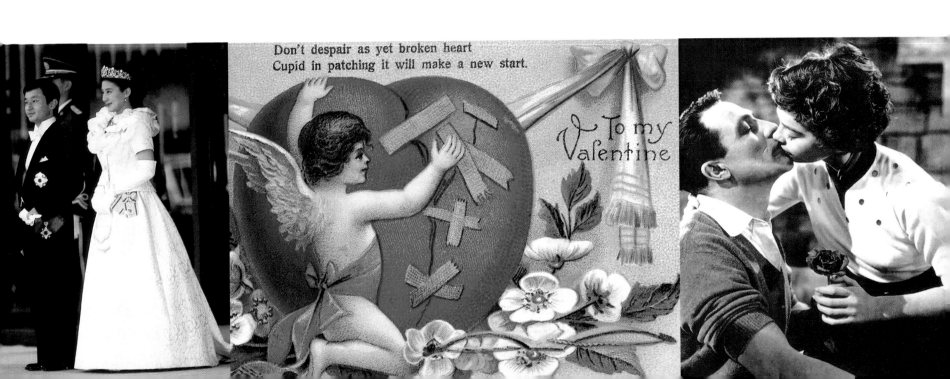

LOVE TOKENS

Without getting into fetishism, lovers of all times and places have given each other presents. From things they make themselves to priceless pieces, from a picture card to precious jewels. Love alone can give value to the slightest trinket.

This couple is quite characteristic of the thirties. Even though the clothing indicates a measure of freedom, the gestures of love seem quite harmless by today's standards.

Half-nude young woman seated on a mound and holding a heart pierced by an arrow. Majolica plate from Faenza (Italy) from around 1500-1510. A fine piece of work. . . .
National Museum of the Renaissance, Ecouen

"Give a kiss, my beauty, only when you are wearing the ring." (Faust by Gounod). Especially if it's richly set with an emerald and plenty of diamonds, as this one is.

The Seasons of Love. Springtime:
emerging love; summer: burning
love; autumn: passionate love;
winter: sincere love. This
deliciously vapid postcard is
representative of the era
between the two world wars.

The Language of the Eyes.
A reflection of the soul and the
heart. A postcard from before 1914.

A box of chocolates, so you
don't arrive empty-handed.

LOVE TOKENS

The language of flowers. For use by the timid.
Postcard from the time between the world wars.

The lady of the manor's bobbin allows the
knight disguised as a shepherd to pay court to
his lady. Lithograph by Saint-Aulaire in the
style of Déveria (Middle Ages).

This postcard from the 1920s
illustrates the song of the heart
in all its stages.

Henry II-era chest with eleven drawers
and, in the center, the fountain of love.
National Museum of the Renaissance, Ecouen.

"Diamonds are a girl's best
friend," sang Marilyn
Monroe in the 1953
Howard Hawks movie
Gentlemen Prefer Blondes.

A bouquet of pink roses like this
one guarantees a tender and
sincere love.

THE LANGUAGE OF FLOWERS

Flowers, for all their innocence, have a language of their own. You merely have to know what to listen for to understand what they're trying to tell us and what they'll communicate to the person who receives them. Just as you wouldn't offer red roses to a very young girl, sending a pot of heather to the woman you hope to marry wouldn't be appropriate.

A bouquet composed primarily of white roses shows the one you adore your sincere love and celebrates her beauty.

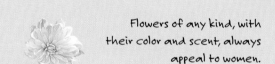

Flowers of any kind, with their color and scent, always appeal to women.

Floral composition of orange roses: orange, a mixture of red and yellow, conveys its meaning in muted colors. It's the type of bouquet you give to a woman you don't yet know very well and to whom you want to show respect.

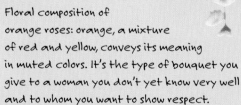

The gradation of the color pink in this rich bouquet unveils love's delicacy.

When florists fill orders for weddings, they can let their imaginations have free rein.

The harmony between pink and yellow in this bouquet communicates a purity of feeling rarely glimpsed.

Little Lexicon of Flowers

ANEMONE	Neglect	HELIOTROPE	Devotion, fidelity	ORCHID	Love, beauty, refinement
ASTER	Refinement, elegance	HONEYSUCKLE	Ambition	PANSY	Affection
AZALEA	Fragile passion	HYACINTH	Physical beauty	PEONY	Timidity
CAMELLIA	Admiration, perfection	IRIS	Promise	PINK ROSE	Tender love
CAMPANULA	Gratitude	IVY	Friendship	POPPY	Remembrance
CARNATION	Caprice, disdain	JASMINE	Friendliness, gaiety	PRIMROSE	Inconstancy, flighty love
CROCUS	Attachment	JONQUIL	Desire, ardent friendship	RED ROSE	Ardent love
DAHLIA	Instability, cheating	LAVENDER	Distrust	ROSEBUD	Young love
DAISY	Innocence	LILAC	First love	SNAPDRAGON	Despair
EDELWEISS	Perseverance	LILY	Purity of heart, virginity	SWEET PEA	Absence
FORGET-ME-NOT	True love	LILY OF THE VALLEY	Tenderness, humility	TULIP	Love
FRENCH MARIGOLD	Jealousy	MAGNOLIA	Love of nature	VIOLET	Modesty, fidelity
FUSCHIA	Grace	MARGUERITE	Innocence, sweetness, discretion	WATER LILY	Purity of heart
GARDENIA	Secret love			WHITE ROSE	Love, beauty, sincerity
GERANIUM	Melancholy	MIMOSA	Overly sensitive	YELLOW ROSE	Jealousy
GLADIOLUS	Combativeness	NARCISSUS	Consideration		
HEATHER	Solitude	NASTURTIUM	Conquest, victory		

Obviously, undecided suitors can order mixed bouquets that will communicate the complexity, the evolution, or the final result of their feelings. . . .

Valentine's Day

So who is this Valentine that lovers celebrate nowadays? Perhaps a Roman priest of the third century, who defied the prohibition by emperor Claudius Gothicus of uniting very young people—for fear that the boy would neglect his military duty—secretly married a couple. For that reason, he was supposedly decapitated, and the commemoration of this martyr was set for the fourteenth of February. It's noteworthy that this love saint is honored around the time of Carnival and the ancient pagan tradition of marking the end of winter and the renewal of nature. This is a fertility rite that is found in one form or another in all civilizations.

"Some believe that Valentine's Day is associated with the Roman Lupercalia."

Other historians affirm that Valentine's Day perpetuates the memory of Charles d'Orléans, a French poet who was taken prisoner in 1415 at the battle of Agincourt. He sent passionate love letters from where he was held in the Tower of London—one of which bore the date of February 14—to Marie de Clèves, whom he would marry when he regained his freedom and who bore him a son, the future king Louis XII.

Still others refer to the *galentin*, from the name of the cavalier that girls in the Middle Ages chose to accompany them when they went out. The cavalier was supposed to give a gift to the girl who chose him. For a long time, the fourteenth of February was the date when girls tried to guess what their future husband would look like. If a robin flew by, they were sure to marry a sailor. A sparrow was the sign of a happy marriage with a poor man, and a goldfinch was the harbinger of a good marriage.

Some believe that Valentine's Day is associated with the Roman Lupercalia. Lupercus, who became subsumed into Pan, was the god of shepherds and flocks. The fifteenth of February, the date of this holiday,

Valentine's Day. Sophie Daumier and Marcel Amont, dressed as characters of Peynet, exchange gifts (1960).

Roses are indispensable accessories for Valentine's Day.

The actress Jeanne Sourza congratulates lovers on Valentine's Day (February 14, 1959).

Right: A couple celebrates Valentine's Day in 1967.

Maxims and Poems

"On Valentine's Day the wheel freezes before the mill."

"For Valentine's Day the magpie flies up into the pine tree; if it doesn't spend the night there, there's no cause for joy."

"Séverin, Valentine, and Faustin freeze everything in their path."

It's Valentine's Day!
I must, but dare not
Tell her in the morning . . .
How awful
Valentine's Day is!
("A Poor Young Shepherd" by Paul Verlaine.)

"It's customary to give a bouquet of flowers or some chocolates to the person you love."

"In recent years, Valentine has regained some favor."

also marked the start of springtime in ancient Rome. On that occasion, there was a random drawing of names of boys and girls who were signed up for the love lottery and who then had to go together for a whole year—or longer—if they suited each other.

In Europe, it's customary to give a bouquet of flowers or some chocolates to the person you love. That pales in comparison to the 900 million Valentines exchanged in the United States on Valentine's Day.

In France, Saint Valentine makes his headquarters in the heart of Berry. Every year, over the weekend that precedes the fourteenth of February, lovers take part in a competition for the greatest kiss. They have the opportunity to plant a tree—cedar, maple, cherry, or apple—on a plot reserved by the town for this purpose. The village of Saint Valentine, with fewer than 300 inhabitants, is the only one in France that bears that name. It offers a special postal cancellation that pictures the lovers of Peynet.

A village in the south of France celebrates another appealing custom to commemorate the arrival of some relics of Saint Valentine more than a century ago. On this occasion, Roquemaure takes on the appearance it had at that time, with an old-style marketplace, horse-drawn carriages, and horseback riders.

Valentine is not so highly esteemed everywhere, though . . . even if he has regained some favor in recent years. As February draws near, you need only pause before the display windows of florists, bakeries, and fashion shops. The heart occupies center stage in the form of bouquets, cakes, and . . . handbags. That's proof, if such were needed, that he has managed to survive through the ages.

Marriage

For a long time, marriage was merely a union of common interests. Nowadays, it seems that for many people it has become the ultimate stage of love.

Exotic marriage in Atlanta, Georgia in the eighties.

"Things have changed a lot, but that doesn't mean marriage has ceased to be a source of stability."

It used to be out of the question to love one another without the authorization of the mayor and the blessing of the priest. Children born out of wedlock were looked down upon as illegitimate. Well and good if the father was a king, prince, or duke, but everyone else became a social outcast. Things have changed a lot, but that doesn't mean that marriage has ceased to be a source of stability. The marriage rate in France is 4.8 marriages per thousand inhabitants. That remained unchanged between 1993 and 1996, even though young people under the age of

Traditional weddings, such as this one in 1993, are still appropriate in Japan; sometimes the bride and groom dress in more modern clothes on this day of celebration.

102

Mais t'aime t la fleu u n'en en su, pa faute.

Cela n'a a mportance, a tu as été que moi. he d'être

Moon bride and her interplanetary husband in their special suits for weightlessness (1962).

A wedding ring for Christmas (1900).

. . . Marriage Stories

"Cats eat outside the dish, and people with spirit make love outside marriage."
(Victor Hugo.)

"They lived happily ever after . . . and they had lots of children."
(Fairy tale.)

". . . Renée's soul was intact, and her body was even more so; marriage seems merely to have changed her girl's virginity into a wife's virginity."
(Jean Giroudoux.)

"Marriage is an impossible thing, and yet the only solution."
(Letter from Alain-Fournier to Jacques Rivière.)

"Marriage, such as it is, is a peculiar thing, but so far nothing better has been invented."
(Amiel, *Intimate Journal*.)

"Nowadays people don't marry very well the first time; they have to try again."
(*The Little Servant* by Alfred Capus.)

"You also need a little enchantment in marriage."
(Jules Supervielle.)

"Whether it's respected or scoffed at, marriage still makes people dream."

"In France, the wedding ring is worn on the left hand; in Spain, on the right; and in India, on a toe."

twenty-five represent only a quarter of newlyweds. Is this due to modern life, to economic difficulties, or to the spirit of the times? It's due to all that and many other things as well. In urban areas, one out of every four marriages ends in divorce. That's enough to discourage good intentions! Just the same, whether it's respected or scoffed at, marriage still makes people dream. Maybe people don't get married for life, but they still get married, especially when there's a baby on the way. Composite families, which are so common nowadays, are proof that what might be regarded as an institution is, in reality, an ambition and a life plan.

The white gown—formerly a mourning dress among French queens—that people like to think of as a symbol of virginity, is no longer the emblem of the "most wonderful day of a woman's life." The fashion has spread all the way to the Far East, where white remains the color of mourning even now. In Japan, the bride slips it on over the traditional kimono and under an evening dress. In Cambodia, the bride and groom change clothes several times in the course of the ceremony. The parents tie the couple's wrists together, probably for fear that one of them will run away. In Mexico, a lasso in the shape of a figure eight is placed around the necks of the couple as a type of wedding ring. Another symbol of marriage is the wedding ring. In France, it's worn on the left hand; in Spain, on the right hand; in India, on a toe—and it's a gift given by the bride's in-laws. Rice in France, rose or marigold petals in India, confetti in China, dates or raisins in Morocco, cumin and coins in Turkey: all these are thrown at the newlyweds. Americans like to throw rice or birdseed when they come out of the church. The Hungarians, who are marvelously pragmatic, sell the guests the right to dance with the bride, and that adds up to a nest egg that's used for the honeymoon! This custom is observed in other eastern European countries as well and in Latin America. Speaking of honeymoons, they figure at the top of wedding lists and well ahead of tea services and silver. Different times, different customs . . .

A pair of young newlyweds during the French Revolution, as seen through the vision of a cinematographer. Stewart Granger and Janet Leigh in *Scaramouche* by George Sidney, 1952.

ANNIVERSARIES

A stone, a metal, a fabric, a tree, a flower—each anniversary has its symbol. Here are some of them:

1 year: paper
5 years: wood
10 years: tin
15 years: crystal
20 years: china
25 years: silver
30 years: pearl
35 years: coral
40 years: ruby
45 years: sapphire
50 years: gold
55 years: emerald
60 years: diamond
65 years: Brazilian
        rosewood
70 years: platinum
75 years: alabaster
80 years: oak

The Lovers' Little Lexicon

ADORATION

The pinnacle of love, feeling love in all your pores, living only for love, yet being eaten away by troubles, caught in a thousand spiders' webs—oh my dear Eva, you have no idea—I have picked up your card, it is before me now, and I am speaking to you as if you were here. I see you as I did yesterday—beautiful, absolutely beautiful. Last night, I kept saying to myself, "She is mine! The angels are not as happy in Paradise as I was yesterday."
Balzac to Ewelina Hanska, January 19, 1834.

"I send you a thousand passionate kisses, I hold you tenderly in my arms, and in my imagination I conjure up different pictures that feature you and me, with nothing and no one else."
Chekov to his wife Olga, August 21, 1901.

LOVERS

"Between lovers there is nothing but blows and caresses."
This Is Man by Suarès.

"A male suitor is always closer to love than to the loved one."
Amphitryon 38 by Jean Giraudoux, 1929.

Lovers, happy lovers,
Do you wish to travel?
Even on domestic shores
You can make a world
That's ever changing, ever new;
To one another be sufficient,
And nothing else will matter.
"The Two Pigeons" by La Fontaine, 1679.

KISS

The most famous kiss. Sculpted in marble in 1886 by Auguste Rodin, *The Kiss*, so realistic and sensual, was still causing scandals in the 1950s,

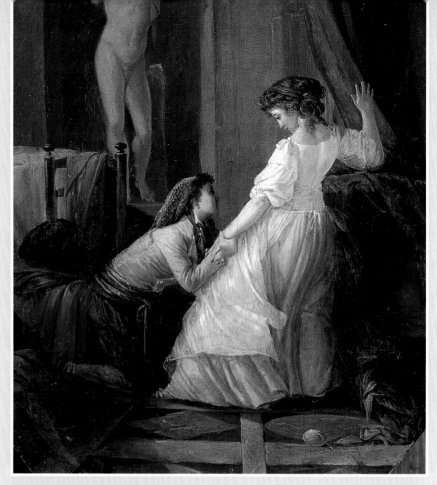

The Declaration by Jean-Baptiste Mallet (1749–1825).
Museum of Fine Arts, Valenciennes.

especially in England.

HAPPINESS

What I want in my house:
A sensible woman,
A cat that mingles with my books,
And friends at all times,
For I can't live without them.
"The Cat" by Guillaume Apollinaire, 1909.

You don't need much to create a world.
You need happiness and nothing else.
Paul Eluard.

Happiness is in the meadow.
Run to get it, run to get it
Happiness is in the meadow.
Run to get it. Before it gets away.
"Happiness" by Paul Fort, 1922.

CELEBRATION

"Love demands everything and rightly so, and that's the way it is with me and you, and with you and me. So close! So far! Isn't it a divine structure, our love—but also as solid as the vault of the heavens!"
Beethoven, perhaps to the countess Giuletta Guicciardi, July 6, 1801.

"O God! For two days I have been asking myself every moment if so much happiness isn't just a dream; it seems that what I am experiencing is no longer of this earth, and I don't understand the beauties of the sky."
Victor Hugo to Adèle Foucher, his future wife, March 15, 1822.

DECLARATION

"I reserved my life for you the moment I laid eyes on you."
Mariana Alcoforado, Portuguese nun, to Noël Bouton de Chamilly, count of Saint-Léger, who abandoned her after seducing her. *Portuguese Letters*, 1668.

"I have something silly and ridiculous to tell you. I am writing it to you stupidly, I'm not sure why, instead of telling it to you at the end of that walk. I'll be sorry tonight. You are going to laugh in my face, take me for a fabricator of phrases in all my dealings with you up to now. You will kick me out and think that I'm lying. I'm in love with you. I have been since the first day I visited you."
Alfred de Musset to George Sand, 1833.

DESIRE

And desire grows when the
*   effect steps back.*
Polyeucte by Corneille, 1642.

When my desires leave by
*   caravan to find you . . .*
The Flowers of Evil by Baudelaire, 1857.

Night is short
And day too long for me.
I flee love and follow its
*   trail,*
You pursue me cruelly, I
*   need your grace,*
I enjoy the torment I
*   endure.*
Sonnet by Joachim Du Bellay, 1550.

DEVOTION

"If I were nothing more than an intelligent woman, I would tell you, my handsome bird, what you most resemble with your feathers and your song! I would tell you that you are the most wonderful of all wonders that have ever existed, and I would be only telling the simple truth."
Juliette Drouet to Victor Hugo, 1835.

Charles Baudelaire

EROTICISM

"Eroticism is acceptance of life even in death."
Literature and Evil by Georges Bataille, 1957.

Yesterday I misspoke, it
*   seems,*
In chatting with
*   Antoinette;*
When I said damn! the little
*   prude*
Made a face and thought
*   me rude,*
And I dropped a bit in her
*   esteem.*
Yet when she turned quite
*   red*

Paul Verlaine

Alphonse de Lamartine

I knew she liked what I had said,
But in some place other than her ear.
Mathurin Régnier (1573–1613)

FLAME
"It seems to me that love must resist all: absence, misfortune, infidelity, and neglect. It's an intimate thing inside us, above us, and at the same time independent from the exterior and the accidents of life . . . no matter what we do, we will always belong to one another; if we should quarrel, we would always come back to one another like rivers that return to their natural beds. You can't escape the destiny of your heart. You belong to me, and I belong to you."
Gustave Flaubert to Louise Colet, November 15, 1846.

INSPIRATION
"I was filled with the tenderness you inspired in me when I appeared among our guests; she was shining in my eyes; she animated my conversations; she controlled my movements; she was evident in everything. They thought me extraordinary, inspired, divine. Grimm could scarcely watch me intently enough or listen to me enough; everyone was astonished; for my part, I felt an inner satisfaction I can't describe. It was like a fire that was burning in the center of my soul and heating my chest, and that spread out over them and set them ablaze. We spent a lively evening and I was the center of it."
Denis Diderot to Sophie Vollant, October 10, 1759.

INSTALLATION
"Dear little woman, I have a number of requests for you: first, I beg you not to be sad; second, to watch out for your health and not trust the spring air; third, not to go out walking alone, and better yet, don't go out at all on foot; fourth, be sure of my love. I have not written you a letter without having your dear portrait in front of me."
Mozart to his wife Constanza, April 16, 1789.

BED
We will have beds filled with light scents. . . .
"The Death of the Lovers" in *The Flowers of Evil* by Baudelaire, 1857.

Jacques Prévert

Guillaume Apollinaire

OBSESSION

"Abandon, opprobrium, and malediction seem to surround me. I came close to killing myself tonight. I wanted to pray, I struck the ground with my forehead, I called for pity from on high, but got none. Perhaps I'm going mad."
Benjamin Constant to Mademoiselle Récamier, September 5, 1815.

POETRY

We are alone
And I sing for you
Freely, joyfully
While only your pure
Voice answers me
It must be time
For this harmony to spread
across

The bleeding ocean
Of these poor years
Where the day is awful
Where the sun's a wound
Where the life of the
universe
Vainly drains away
It must be time my
Madeleine
To weigh the anchor!
Guillaume Apollinaire to Madeleine Pagès, 1915.

POSSESSION

"I am thoroughly penetrated with the happiness that's mine in having you—nothing else counts. You are mine, my precious little everything, my little beloved—today as well as the day before yesterday when I saw you, and I will have you as long as you live—after that, nothing matters much in anything that can happen to me. Not only am I not sad, but rather profoundly happy and self-assured—even the most tender memories of your dear face and little arms around the pillow in the morning are sweet to me. I feel totally enveloped and sustained by your love."
Simone de Beauvoir to Jean-Paul Sartre, 1940.

FIRST TIME

"*Mother! . . . I feel like I could die,*"
she said aloud.
That's because it's the first time, Madame, and the best one.
Paul-Jean Toulet.

REVELATION

"I felt like I was participating in some celebration at once unknown, new, mysterious,

Louis Aragon

and eternal. . . . There was no space, nor time, nor words . . . but infinity, love, forgetfulness, voluptuousness, and charity! In short, God . . . The God my soul longs to find . . . as despair and an excess of pain sometimes presage . . . an all-loving and all-powerful God. . . ."
Franz Liszt to Marie d'Agoult, May 18, 1834.

VIRTUE

Virtue doesn't hold much sway in love.
Songs by Clément Marot.

Couple Kissing
Eighteenth-century painting
showing the sensual side of love.

expressions of love

Gestures of Love

"To speak of love is to make love," wrote Balzac in 1829 in *The Physiology of Marriage*, one of his very first works. Just the same, you can't take that too literally. For even though some of his novels seem to be an illustration of that axiom, the situation is quite the opposite for many others. Besides, it would have occurred to nobody in the nineteenth century, because of the superficial prudishness that reigned during that time, to give their stamp of approval to that statement—except for a few contrary people. A blushing young girl, freshly released from a convent and sometimes accompanied by a duenna responsible for guarding against the slightest misstep, was trained exclusively to make a fine marriage and produce children for her husband. During that time, French bourgeois society relied on contemporary church morality.

"Nowadays people have no qualms about displaying their feelings for all to see."

However, behind the conventions, everything was possible, of course, out of public view. That gave rise to the excessively modest displays that prevailed up to the middle of the twentieth century. Embraces, kisses, and any allusion to pleasure were officially banished from the conduct of lovers—for girls and women, at least, since gallant adventures and sexual exploits were always acclaimed and even encouraged for men.

In our time, to paraphrase Balzac, people talk about it and do it. Without shame or false modesty, and whether boy or girl. Whether they are madly in love or simply attracted to the other person. People also go so far as to display their feelings for all to see, by gestures that a short while ago were reserved for the strictest intimacy.

Illustration for *Memoir of Two Young Lovers*, a novel by Honoré de Balzac. Engraving from 1879.

Mars and Venus, engraving based on Nicolas Poussin (1594–1665). War is put on hold during times of loving.

A Lesson in Conjugal Union based on Louis Lópold Boilly (1761–1845).
National Library of France, Paris.

"Caresses, at first timid and then daring, are part of the love ritual."

People no longer hesitate to embrace or kiss in public places, and they do so without drawing any condemnation from others. When people put their arms around each other, it's no longer considered a sign of debauchery and depravation. Conceiving a child out of wedlock is part of the natural order of things. Or nearly so.

Before we get to that point, there are some other gestures that come into play, and some of them are important indeed. While keeping in mind the definition of the word *gesture* as found in the dictionary—"movement of the hand, arm, or body"—what more is there to say other than that it's an approach and an attempt to gain approval and "possession" of the other person? Caresses, at first timid and then daring, and ultimately audacious, are part of the love ritual. "Between lovers, there is nothing but blows and caresses," wrote Suarès in *This Is Man.* Let's opt for caresses, which are perfectly expressive of a feeling that's at once simple and complex.

In former times, embracing and intertwining in public were considered to be audacious, even indecent. People had to be content with flirting genteelly; going any further risked proscription. "Christianity did a lot for love by making it a sin," wrote Anatole France in 1894 in *The Epicurean's Garden.* Catholics weren't the only ones who were shocked by conduct whose real intent was perfectly clear. A girl who made a mistake was banished from society; only marriage authorized the act of love.

The liberation of morals, accompanied by a fading of religion and the arrival of contraception (at least in our latitudes), certainly did devalue the act. They also removed the taboo, and in the final analysis, they restored loving to the realm of love. Pleasure is a recognized and justifiable value. The dream of lovers, which is to communicate by heart and body, has become a reality. That's a good move on the part of Cupid, that naughty little god who, after all, does just as he pleases!

The Embrace by Carl Binder (end of the nineteenth century/start of the twentieth) expresses the sensuality of love.

Mi corazon

mon lapin

НАДЕЖДА

TERMS OF ENDEARMENT AND SWEET TALK

Sweet talk and terms of endearment are part and parcel of expressing love. Some may seem obsolete, while others are frankly ridiculous and frequently meaningless, except for the people involved. It doesn't matter who makes them up or understands them. My turtle dove, my . . . , my . . . : the imagination of lovers is inexhaustible. Animals provide a constant source of inspiration, too.

mon coin de paradis

σε ἀγαπῶ

عزيزتي
حبيبي

mon ange

Ti voglio tanto bene

Sweet heart

ma poule

МОЙ ГОЛУБЧИК

Ich liebe dich

حَبِّي

I love you

Amore mio

ma colombe mon toit mon canard

당신을 사랑합니다

Я ТЕБЯ ЛЮБЛЮ

Mi sei molto cara

Te quiero

Ma Puce

Mon sucre d'orge

THE KISS

In the twentieth century, the kiss—preferably a passionate one—is the very symbol of love, magnified by poetry, painting, sculpture, and the movies.

Lips avid for colors
And the kisses that sketch it
Flame leaf languid water
A wing holds them in its palm
A laugh knocks them over

Paul Eluard

Leaving Class (1938).
"A kiss, but what is it after all?
A vow made up close,
a promise made more precise, a confession
that seeks confirmation, the word *love*
underlined in pink.
It's a secret that uses the mouth for an ear."
Cyrano de Bergerac by Edmond Rostand, 1897.

Springtime by Louis Henri Nicot (1878–1944). Salon of 1913. "Human love is distinguished from the brutish rut of animals by just two divine functions: the caress and the kiss." *Aphrodite* by Pierre Louÿs.

Marcello Mastroianni and Anita Ekberg in *La Dolce Vita* by Federico Fellini (1960).

The Stolen Kiss by Jean-Baptiste Regnault (1754–1829), based on Fragonard.

National Library of France.

"A legal kiss is never as valuable as a stolen kiss"— confession of a female character of Guy de Maupassant (1850–1893).

An enthusiastic kiss in *Corsair* (Roland West, 1931) between Chester Morris and Allison Lloyd.

The longest kiss in the history of the movies lasts three minutes and fifteen seconds in a second-rate film entitled *You're in the Army Now*, with Jane Wyman and Regis Toomy. Next is the one in *Notorious* by Alfred Hitchcock, followed by this most famous one in *From Here to Eternity* (below) with Burt Lancaster and Deborah Kerr (1953).

Index

PHOTO CREDITS

Front cover: Archives Street. **Back cover:** (t) Archives Street, (b) Sunset.
Cover photo: Humphrey Bogart and Lauren Bacall, celebrated couple in the movies and in real life, on vacation aboard a sailboat in the 1940s.
Photo for back cover: Lovers on a public bench at the Père Lachaise Cemetery in Paris in 1955.

LEGEND

b = bottom, bc = bottom center, bkg = background, bl = bottom left, br = bottom right, c = center, cl = center left, ins = inset, l = left, lm = left middle, m = middle, r = right, t = top, tc = top center, tl = top left, tr = top right

OPENING PHOTOS

pp. 6–7: *Birth of Venus* by Alesander Cabanel (1823–1889), Orsay Museum, Paris; pp. 34–35: *Notorious* by Alfred Hitchcock, with Ingrid Bergman and Cary Grant (1946); pp. 62–63: *The Temple of Love* by Auguste Garneray (1785–1824); Château de Malmaison and Bois-Préau; pp. 88–89: Fantasy postcard picturing a pair of lovers from the Belle-Epoque period.

Conceived and produced by Copyright for Solar Editions
Graphic design: Ute-Charlotte Hettler
Cover: Claire Brenier
Design: Nicole Leymarie
Editorial coordination: Julie Pinon
Editorial collaboration: Janine Trotereau
Translated from the French by Eric A. Bye, M.A.